America's Best Cancer Doctors and Their Secrets

A patient's guide to making an informed choice

by Frank Cousineau

with Andrew Scholberg

America's Best Cancer Doctors and Their Secrets

A patient's guide to making an informed choice

By Frank Cousineau with Andrew Scholberg

Published by Online Publishing & Marketing, LLC

A Publication from *Cancer Defeated!*

IMPORTANT CAUTION:

By reading this special report, you are demonstrating an interest in maintaining good and vigorous health.

This report suggests ways you can do that, but — as with anything in medicine — there are no guarantees.

You must check with private, professional medical advisors to assess whether the suggestions in this report are appropriate for you. And please note, the contents of this report may be considered controversial by the medical community at large.

The authors, editors and publishers of this report are not doctors or professional health caregivers. They have relied on information from people who are. The information in this report is not meant to replace the attention or advice of physicians or other healthcare professionals. Nothing contained in this report is intended to constitute personal medical advice for any particular individual.

Every reader who wishes to begin any dietary, drug, exercise or other lifestyle changes intended to treat a specific disease or health condition should first get the advice of a qualified health care professional.

No alternative OR mainstream cancer treatment can boast a one hundred percent record of success. Far from it. There is ALWAYS some risk involved in any cancer treatment. The authors, editors, and publishers of this report are not responsible for any adverse effects or results from the use of any of the suggestions, preparations or procedures described in this report. As with any medical treatment, results of the treatments described in this report will vary among individuals.

PLEASE DO NOT USE THIS REPORT IF YOU ARE NOT WILLING TO ASSUME THE RISK.

The authors report here the results of a vast array of experiments and research as well as the personal experiences of individual patients, health care professionals and caregivers. In most cases the authors were not present themselves to witness the events but relied on the accounts of people who were.

ISBN 978-1-4951-1653-7

Printed in the United States of America.

ABOUT THE AUTHORS

Frank Cousineau is a California-based researcher, author, and consultant in the field of alternative health. He is also the president of two nonprofit organizations devoted to informing cancer patients about effective alternative therapies and helping them take advantage of those therapies.

Frank's interest in alternative health was aroused in 1973 when his mother developed cancer for the third time in 17 years. The futile attempts of his mother's doctors to arrest the disease frustrated Frank, and led him to launch a lifelong quest to identify effective natural alternatives to conventional cancer treatment.

Over the last 35 years, Frank has visited 6 countries and logged more than 150,000 miles to investigate dozens of treatments and clinics. In the process, he's been among the first researchers to inform Americans about health breakthroughs that have improved and saved lives.

His years of research have made him a prized consultant to physicians and clinics seeking information about alternative and complementary cancer treatments. He has also organized and conducted more than 80 consumer tours of North American alternative cancer clinics. Many cancer patients who join the tours return to the clinics and are successfully treated.

When Frank isn't traveling the world seeking out new treatments and first-rate clinics, he lives in Modesto, California with his wife Chayo, and enjoys spending time with his children and grandchildren. Frank and Chayo also run Life Support, which supplies nutritional supplements to physicians.

Andrew Scholberg is a freelance writer living in Florida as well as a devotee of alternative medicine. He is the author of ***German Cancer Breakthrough*** and the co-author, with Frank Cousineau, of ***The Amish Cancer Secret***. He was the defendant in a landmark First Amendment case before the Supreme Court that was ultimately decided in his favor. In his spare time, Andrew is an adventurous outdoorsman.

Table Of Contents

Chapter One

The little-known American doctors who defeat cancer — despite danger of persecution

Few Americans know this, but doctors at a few hidden clinics in America are routinely helping patients get rid of cancer — even so-called "hopeless" and "terminal" cancer. In this Special Report I'm going to tell you all about these rare doctors that only a few people know about.

You're probably wondering why this information is secret and why hardly any of these doctors advertise that they can defeat cancer. I can tell you exactly why these special clinics are hidden and rare.

The shocking answer is this: We no longer have health freedom in this country. Maybe you think America is still a free country.

Dr. James Forsythe, M.D., endured a Gestapo-style raid on his home by armed agents of the federal government who pulled into his driveway in three black SUVs as he and his wife were enjoying coffee after breakfast. Dr. David Steenblock, D.O., has been harassed. So has Dr. Frank Shallenberger, M.D.

More recently the federal government raided the Camelot cancer clinic in Tulsa, Oklahoma, shortly after we toured it in 2013. Many of the doctors in this report have been persecuted or hassled.

Why America's best-known holistic doctor doesn't accept cancer patients

One of the doctors I interviewed for this Special Report is Julian Whitaker, M.D., the founder of the Whitaker Wellness Institute in Newport Beach, California.

Dr. Whitaker, who's probably the best-known holistic doctor in America, doesn't accept cancer patients because of the hostile political climate surrounding cancer treatment. Instead, he refers cancer patients elsewhere. He told me he doesn't want to practice medicine with a bullseye painted on his back.

In this Special Report you'll learn the name of the alternative clinic to which Dr. Whitaker refers cancer patients.

I'm going to tell you about alternative cancer treatments that are hard to find in America. These treatments produce extraordinary recoveries from cancer. Some of these recoveries are so spectacular that people call them miracles. And I'm going to tell you which American doctors stand at the very top of the medical profession worldwide in the treatment of cancer.

Let me explain why I wrote this Special Report.

You see, my own Mom died of cancer. She struggled with it — on and off — from 1956 till her death in 1973. This was an agonizing ordeal not just for Mom but also for our whole family.

In 1956 the doctors recommended a pan-hysterectomy for her uterine cancer. In plain English, they wanted to remove her uterus and both ovaries. She underwent this drastic operation, and she seemed to be well.

But her cancer snuck back 10 years later, appearing as full-blown colon cancer. The doctors again recommended drastic surgery: the removal of a large portion of her colon. After that ordeal she was never the same again.

Chemo caused my Mom to retch so violently she said, 'No more chemo, ever again!'

Then in 1973 the doctors told her she had an "advanced" case of cancer. They recommended a form of chemo that's still widely used today. The chemo didn't just make her vomit; it made her retch violently. It was so harsh she said she'd rather die than undergo one more round of it. She kept sliding downhill until she died.

Fortunately, if you or your loved ones ever get cancer, you don't have to go through the same drastic, painful, and futile treatment my Mom suffered through.

If you ordered this Special Report because you're seeking hope for a loved one or for yourself, I'm going to give you a bright ray of hope.

After my Mom died of cancer I embarked on a quest to find out if something could have been done to save her. I didn't want to see any of my other loved ones waste away and die of this horrible, dreaded disease.

I believe the information in this report would have saved my Mom

My quest led me to become involved in the alternative health movement. For more than 30 years, I've volunteered my time with two California-based not-for-profit organizations that assist cancer patients and provide information about alternative cancer treatments.

Through my volunteer work I've become friends with some of the finest physicians in America and in the world — doctors who are turning around "hopeless" and "terminal" cancers.

In fact, if I'd had the information I'm about to share with you when my Mom learned she had cancer, I believe she would've died years later of old age instead.

I know the alternative doctors' scientific insights, methods, clinics, treatment options, and track records. I have more connections with alternative cancer doctors and clinics in America and abroad than perhaps anyone else in the alternative health movement.

In this Special Report, I'll recommend only the doctors and clinics I know to be outstanding.

The medical establishment is lying about your cancer treatment options

You see, I have a passion for alternative health and a passion for the truth. Not long after my Mom's death I discovered that the American medical establishment isn't telling Americans the truth about cancer and the treatment options.

Basically, the American medical establishment offers three treatment choices: surgery, radiation, and chemotherapy. In other words, you can choose to get cut, burned, or poisoned.

But as I'll show you in this Special Report, many other effective treatment options exist. And unlike the conventional treatments, the best cancer treatments deal with *the root causes of cancer*. And these treatments don't have the dreadful side-effects associated with chemo and radiation, such as nausea, vomiting, and hair loss.

In my opinion and that of the most successful alternative cancer doctors, a tumor is only a symptom that something in your body has gone haywire. That's why tumors so often grow back after conventional treatments by American doctors.

For more than 30 years I've seen people come to alternative clinics and — their cancers disappear. The treatments they receive have been proven to help. These former cancer patients might die 10 or 20 years later of cardiovascular disease or something else, but their cancer is GONE!

My colleague Andrew Scholberg and I interviewed the following doctors:

- Dr. Donna Abfall, N.D.
- Dr. Ferre Akbarpour, M.D.
- Dr. Kent Bartell, D.C.

- Dr. Tim Birdsall, N.D.
- Dr. Jeoff Drobot, N.M.D.
- Dr. Robert Eslinger, D.O., H.M.D.
- Dr. James W. Forsythe, M.D., H.M.D.
- Dr. Carlos Garcia, M.D.
- Dr. Colleen Huber, N.M.D.
- Dr. Lynn Jennings, M.D.
- Dr. Lance Morris, N.M.D.
- Dr. Richard Olson, D.C.
- Dr. James Privitera, M.D. (deceased)
- Dr. Charles Schwengel, D.O., D.O.H.
- Dr. Frank Shallenberger, M.D., H.M.D.
- Dr. O. Carl Simonton, M.D. (deceased)
- Dr. David Steenblock, D.O.
- Dr. Phranq Tamburri, N.M.D.
- Dr. Dickson Thom, D.D.S., N.D.
- Dr. Renee Welhouse, N.D., Ph.D. (deceased)
- Dr. Julian Whitaker, M.D.

Let me explain the initials. M.D. stands for Medical Doctor, of course. N.D. stands for Naturopathic Doctor, N.M.D. stands for Naturopathic Medical Doctor, D.O. stands for Doctor of Osteopathy, D.O.H. stands for Doctor of Osteopathy and Homeopathy, and D.C. stands for Doctor of Chiropractic.

What about Cancer Treatment Centers of America?

Perhaps you've seen the advertisements for the Cancer Treatment Centers of America (CTCA). These centers are located in or near several major American cities, and CTCA's advertisements claim to offer a combination of conventional cancer treatments and some natural therapies such as nutritional support, mind-body medicine, and spiritual support.

We give CTCA credit for publishing their treatment results, which are better than the results of conventional cancer treatment *alone*. If you want conventional cancer treatment, choosing CTCA would give you a better chance of survival because of the natural therapies they add to conventional treatment.

But we don't include a chapter about CTCA in this book and wouldn't choose CTCA ourselves because we believe CTCA is heavily tilted toward conventional treatment. This heavy tilt means they have no collegial relationship with the most outstanding integrative/holistic cancer physicians in America – a lack of collegiality that's unfortunate.

URGENT warning about PET/CT scanners

We're also concerned about CTCA's use of PET/CT scanners for diagnostic imaging. One of America's top integrative cancer doctors, James Forsythe, M.D., H.M.D., of Reno, Nevada, told us that PET/CT scans are over-used. He recommends that patients stay as far away as possible from PET/CT scanners because he says they emit 500 to 600 times the radiation dose of a simple chest X-ray. This radiation beats down the patient's immune cells, which are radio sensitive.

Dr. Forsythe told us that major hospitals such as the Mayo Clinic and M.D. Anderson want cancer patients to have a PET/CT scan every three months just to see how the therapy is doing. "This is self-defeating, and they don't get it," said Dr. Forsythe.

He also criticizes conventional cancer hospitals that provide soft drinks and a big bowl of candy in their infusion centers so that cancer patients can get sugared up. Cancer doctors should know that sugar *feeds* cancer!

We're also concerned about the exorbitant cost of conventional treatment at CTCA. This cost may be no big deal for those who have adequate health insurance, but few people without health insurance can afford a six-figure medical bill.

In sharp contrast, the clinics we recommend in this special report charge far less than CTCA, Sloan-Kettering, M.D. Anderson, Mayo, and other hospitals that offer conventional treatments. And the good news is that the less expensive treatments are more effective. If you're interested in statistics that bear that out, read the chapters about Dr. Colleen Huber and Dr. James Forsythe, both of whom have gathered impressive statistics on the outcomes of their treatments.

Some pros and cons of your cancer treatment options

Let me summarize your four basic treatment options for cancer.

1. The conventional treatment: surgery, radiation, and chemotherapy
2. The conventional treatment PLUS the mind-body methods developed by the late Dr. O. Carl Simonton, M.D., which we describe in Chapter 11.
3. Nontoxic alternative (holistic) treatments that build up your immune system and rid your body of toxins
4. An "integrative" or complementary approach that includes both conventional and holistic therapies

If you choose option number one, it's true that you might survive, particularly if the cancer is early-stage. With late stage cancer, your odds of success plummet if you rely exclusively on conventional treatment.

As Dr. Julian Whitaker, M.D., told us, radiation and chemotherapy are "dangerous placebos." Placebos sometimes work, but the risks of toxic therapies are obvious. They can certainly kill the cancer. But they sometimes kill the patient, too.

If you're thinking about surgery, you should know that cancer surgeries carry a greater risk of certain complications than do similar surgeries on patients who don't have cancer. A cancer patient incurs at least twice the risk of postoperative deep vein thrombosis (DVT) and more than three times the risk of fatal pulmonary embolism than non-cancer patients who have similar procedures.

Option number two – conventional treatment plus mind-body methods – gives you a much better chance of survival than option number one. Statistics prove this through sound scientific studies, as you'll see in the chapter about Dr. Simonton's mind-body methods.

I believe options three and four give cancer patients an excellent chance of survival. No clinic, doctor, or course of treatment can guarantee that *every* cancer patient will survive. There is always a risk of failure, and the patient must be prepared to assume that risk if he or she decides to try the treatments described in the coming chapters. But the information in this Special Report can help put the odds in your favor and give you a better quality of life as well.

How much do the various cancer treatments cost?

If you choose nontoxic treatments, alternative clinics usually charge about $3,000 to $4,000 per week on the low end and about $10,000 or more per week on the high end. Treatment at an alternative clinic typically lasts about three weeks, but stubborn cases of cancer may require a longer course of treatment. Medical insurance generally doesn't pay for such nontoxic treatments.

If you choose conventional treatments, your medical bills will hit six figures so fast it will make your head spin. It costs as much as $850,000 to die of cancer in America, by the time you add up all the costs of surgery, radiation, chemo, MRIs, hospitalization, and so on. Insurance usually does pay most of the bill for conventional treatments, but even the small amount that's NOT covered can bankrupt you.

It's puzzling that insurance companies aren't willing to cover less expensive treatments that are more effective. Perhaps they're uninformed about the alternative treatments. More likely, they're prisoners of the medical mainstream consensus.

You're responsible for your decisions about health care, and no one can make them for you. You can call your own shots. But no matter what option or clinic you choose, after you've read the chapter about Dr. Simonton's pioneering work, you'll almost certainly want to add his mind-body methods to your treatment program.

Some of the doctors profiled in this Special Report have had astonishing success in using nontoxic therapies ONLY — no chemo, drugs, or radiation whatsoever. Others use an integrative, complementary approach, which you might call "the best of both worlds."

The complementary approach, which uses alternative AND conventional therapies, is remarkably effective. A surprising benefit is that good nutritional support enables patients to endure chemo and radiation with fewer problems. The same is true of Dr. Simonton's mind-body methods.

Medical wisdom of the ages

All of the holistic doctors we profile in this Special Report have a profound respect for the healing power of the human body. One of the greatest physicians of all time, Paracelsus (1493-1541), advised:

"Follow nature, and she will be your instructor. The ways of nature are simple, and she does not require any complicated prescriptions. The invisible forces in the body are powerful and may be guided by the imagination and propelled by the will."

Chapter Two

The professor and student team up to offer the treatment of the future

Having visited 37 holistic cancer clinics in five countries, I can say that you'd be hard pressed to find a clinic with a more impressive array of diagnostic and therapeutic machines than the American Center for Biological Medicine in Scottsdale, Arizona.

Two remarkable doctors have teamed up to create a model for the medical treatment of the future. One of them is Dr. Dickson Thom, a former professor at a medical school in Portland, Oregon. The other is Dr. Jeoff Drobot, who was one of Dr. Thom's most brilliant students – one he remembers as a voracious reader.

Diagnostic tests pinpoint hidden problems

To help me better understand what the typical patient goes through at the clinic, Dr. Drobot gave me some of the key diagnostic tests he and his partner give to the patients. [Editor's note: These tests were done on co-author Andrew Scholberg, not on the author, Frank Cousineau.]

One test measured 119 acupuncture points on my upper body twice: before *and* after stress. After doing the first measurement, my body was stressed by being put in a cold room for a few minutes. This test showed the strength or weakness of every organ in my body. Another test measured the flexibility of my arteries. Other tests evaluated my nervous system, digestive system, lymphatic system, cardiopulmonary system, and other systems.

The testing took about an hour, and I was astonished at the information it provided about my health. There was no evidence of disease, but the tests identified a couple of issues that Dr. Drobot said are easily correctable. He recommended that I follow the three-week detox eating plan described in *The Swiss Secret* by Thomas Rau, M.D., the director of the legendary Paracelsus clinic in Lustmühle, Switzerland.

I happen to know Dr. Rau, having interviewed him when I visited Paracelsus on my last tour of cancer clinics in Europe. Paracelsus is one of the top holistic clinics in the world. Dr. Drobot, too, has spent time at the Paracelsus Clinic to learn about its diagnostic and therapeutic techniques.

In fact, he and Dr. Thom have traveled widely to discuss cancer treatment with doctors at some of the most outstanding holistic clinics. That's one way they find out about the most effective treatments and apply them at the American Center for Biological Medicine.

It's like the Paracelsus Clinic in Switzerland

As Dr. Thom told me, "We believe that in the US and Canada we have the most comprehensive collection of diagnostic and therapeutic machineries – both from the US and from European technology. The Paracelsus Clinic in Switzerland has similar types of things. We don't have anything unique. But there's no clinic that has this entire collection.

"We have machines that increase electrons,

machines that increase oxygenation of cells, hyperthermia for detox, cryotherapy for metabolic stimulation and nervous system reboot, colonic hydrotherapy for detox, ozone therapy, rectal implants for probiotics, sound beds and other machines for parasympathetic/sympathetic nervous system balancing, IV therapies for uplifting nutrients, and a comprehensive array of diagnostic machines.

"That's why we call ourselves the American Center for Biological Medicine. There are biological medicine centers that do bits and pieces of this. But there's no other American clinic that has accumulated the therapies we offer here – which also include our supplements and our homeopathic treatments and energetic therapies. We still have about 10 machines sitting in cupboards that we haven't cracked open yet because we haven't yet decided how to incorporate them into our practice."

Dr. Thom remarked, "We also have a garage full of junk. We paid thousands for it and tried it, but it didn't work. But a lot of the stuff we bought *did* work."

The machines Dr. Thom and Dr. Drobot use have passed a strict litmus test: they're *consistently* useful and effective. Best of all, when a patient repeats the diagnostic tests after a week or two of treatment, the measurable improvement in the test results gives the patient objective proof that the treatment is actually working. This proof gives patients a big boost of confidence that they're on the road to health, which also helps the healing process.

Hyperthermia is available!

During my tour of the clinic, Dr. Drobot told me that he likes to use technology because it gets a much faster result than nutritional supplements. His clinic is one of the few in America that offers hyperthermia – a treatment that gives the patient an artificial fever for about two hours. The induced fever tells the immune system to wake up and get busy – just like a natural fever.

Hyperthermia also kills or weakens cancer cells. This heat therapy, which was perfected in Germany, is hard to find in America. Dr. Drobot said, "Hyperthermia is great because it makes up for lost time. You see an increased reaction in the patient."

The clinic's hyperthermia machine consists of heating pads above and below the patient that raise the patient's body temperature above 100 degrees Fahrenheit. The doctors at this clinic give an extra "kick" to hyperthermia by adding photons and magnetic fields. Dr. Drobot remarked, "You can do these three treatments at once."

He calls the clinic's treatments "re-stimulation therapies." He said, "We treat the *patient*, and you need lots of tools in the tool box because everybody is different. One person's cancer is different from another person's cancer." Hyperthermia is only one of many such tools at the clinic.

This machine beats hyperbaric oxygen ten-fold

Dr. Drobot showed me the oxygen therapy room, which contains five different machines that work in various ways to get oxygenation back into the system. Cancer hates oxygen.

One machine in particular impressed me: the high altitude oxygen machine, which Dr. Drobot said is "10 to 20 times better than hyperbaric oxygen chambers." He explained, "It's like a super duper EWOT therapy." EWOT, as you may know, stands for "exercise with oxygen therapy."

He added, "I like to have as many different tools as I can. I can flush out lactic acid fast and pump oxygen back into the cell, and it lasts for about three days. We put a great deal of oxygen back in the patient's plasma. We also do ozone therapy. There are many ways to load tissues up with oxygen, and they're all important." I'd never seen anything like the high altitude oxygen machine.

The "cryo-sauna": A possible therapeutic breakthrough

Another therapy that astonished me is cryotherapy, also known as the "cryo-sauna," which is the extreme polar opposite of hyperthermia. Cryotherapy uses liquid nitrogen to expose the patient to a temperature of 150 degrees below zero Fahrenheit for three minutes. I told Dr. Drobot, "I've never seen anything like that, either."

"You won't," he replied. "It's very cold for three minutes, which re-stimulates the nervous system and chases the blood flow into the core, giving the patient six hours of increased blood flow. It also stimulates the immune cells. It's excellent for healing and for repair. You won't find another treatment like that."

When he first described cryotherapy I was bewildered. I wondered how could a patient in nothing but socks and underwear tolerate a temperature of 150 degrees below zero for three minutes? I asked Dr. Drobot to explain how this is even possible without being harmful or intolerable.

He replied, "It sounds way worse than it is. It's *short bursts* of extreme cold. The cold comes in three-second spurts, and that gives the patient the metabolic stimulation and nervous system regeneration that's needed. You just can't do it with anything else. It's the most effective thing I've found. The patient needs the autonomic nervous systems to be back so that cells communicate, and this is the most effective way to do it!"

Then Dr. Drobot showed me the clinic's collection of machines that move the lymph – a key part of detoxification. He said, "We use a bunch of machines for this. When we strip out the lymphatic system we saturate it with oxygen and electrons because it helps when you have oxygen and electrons in there." In one therapy, powerful suction cups bring lymphatic fluid to the surface to burn off some of the garbage in the lymphatic fluid.

Dr. Drobot let me try one of the machines that move lymph. A clinic employee placed two magnetic wands on my chest and two more on my legs and then turned on the machine. The wands have a magnetic force that's ten times more effective than manual lymphatic drainage. It only took about 20 minutes. Dr. Drobot reiterated, "I like to use technology because it's faster."

Dr. Drobot said their clinic has "tons" of intravenous (IV) therapies. Each patient's disease is unique, and the IV therapies are individualized for each patient.

The clinic has two "sound beds" – beds that allow the technician to "dial the phone number" of any organ's frequency to stimulate it. The sound bed also helps the patient relax, which activates the patient's parasympathetic nervous system. The parasympathetic state is essential for recovery from cancer. I tried out the sound bed and found it completely relaxing.

These doctors empower their patients to regain health

The 7,000-square-foot clinic also contains a classroom, which the doctors use to educate and empower patients to take charge of their health. My friend and colleague Bill Henderson, the author of the popular book *Cancer-Free*, has been to the clinic more than once to make presentations in the its classroom. The American Center for Biological Medicine is one of Bill's favorite clinics.

The clinic uses a "closed system" colonic hydrotherapy machine, which Dr. Drobot considers more thorough and effective than the "open" kind. He explained, "It's easier to add implantation of probiotics when you have a closed system."

When we came to Dr. Dickson Thom's office, Dr. Drobot introduced us and then told me, "Show Dick your lab results. Dick will give you a scolding. Let's see if he comes up with the same things I told you. Then you'll know we're legit." We all laughed because Dr. Thom is mild, easygoing, and friendly, sort of like Marcus Welby, M.D.

Though these two doctors can write prescriptions for any drug at the pharmacy, they prefer to use natural medicine. Dr. Drobot told me that the prescription pad on his desk remains unused because "every drug comes with some kind of problem," and he has learned how to get fast results without drugs.

Dr. Thom told me he didn't start his medical career to become a cancer doctor. It happened because he felt an obligation to help whoever walked through his clinic's door.

Oncologist asks colleagues: "How can this patient *still* be alive?"

One of Dr. Thom's patients had been diagnosed in 1998 with a rare and deadly cancer: mantle cell lymphoma. The man had already undergone a bone marrow transplant. In 2002 the man's oncologist gave him a grim prognosis, telling him, "You shouldn't have had the bone marrow transplant because we now realize it doesn't work. Your life expectancy is about two years. We can give you a palliative drug, which will give you relief for six to eight weeks. When we give you the drug again, the relief will be shorter. Get your affairs in order."

Desperate for a healing miracle, the patient came to Dr. Thom, who rolled up his sleeves and treated him aggressively with natural therapies. Six or eight weeks later he returned to the conventional doctor who'd given him the palliative drug. The doctor said, "Your numbers look pretty good, so let's just wait before giving you another dose of the drug."

The man kept on going back to the conventional doctor every couple of months for evaluation, but his numbers continued to look good. In fact, his numbers were so good that he never did need a second dose of the palliative drug. He was free of cancer.

In 2006, the oncologist went to a medical conference to present this extraordinary case. He asked his colleagues how a patient diagnosed in 1998 with mantle cell lymphoma could *still* be alive eight years later. They had no answer. As far as any of them knew, he was the longest surviving mantle cell lymphoma patient in the world. In fact, the man is still alive several years later and in good health today.

Oncologist defers to Dr. Thom!

The patient's oncologist found out that he'd been doing natural therapies with Dr. Thom but was open minded about it. He told the patient, "Just do whatever Dr. Thom tells you to do because I don't know what he's doing. I don't know his remedies. I don't know anything about his therapies, but it's working, and I have nothing to offer you." This oncologist deserves commendation for having the humility to admit what he doesn't know.

Dr. Thom says, "More and more cancer patients started showing up because my cancer patients were feeling better. Did they live forever? No. Of course not. But just about all of them outlive the prediction given them by conventional doctors."

Ironically, Dr. Thom says he doesn't treat cancer and doesn't know how to treat it. Yet he's skilled at helping patients beat cancer – even one of the deadliest cancers known to man – a type of cancer that stumps conventional doctors. He accomplished this by applying what he knows: he treats the <u>patient</u> and focuses on optimizing the patient's *health*.

Cancer patients desperately need detoxification, immune boosting therapies, oxygenation, and nutritional support. As the patient becomes healthier and stronger, cancer becomes weaker.

Dr. Drobot compares health to a bucket full of water. If the bucket develops any kind of hole, it must be fixed if the bucket is to hold water. When evaluating a sick patient, Dr. Drobot and his partner try to identify the "leaks" that are causing the disease. Using sophisticated diagnostic technology, they look at every organ, the nervous system, the endocrine system, the immune system, the circulatory system, the digestive system, and so on, to see where the problem is.

Here's yet another way to look at it. The problems that cause cancer are like anchors that pull the patient down. These anchors include dental problems, emotional problems, mercury, environmental toxicity, unrelieved stress, and so on. The doctors are skilled at identifying these anchors, and they have effective therapies to get rid of them.

Severe stress feeds cancer

In the typical cancer patient, the nervous system is out of balance. This is understandable because a cancer diagnosis is guaranteed to cause major stress. A bleak prognosis adds to the distress. But unrelieved stress impairs digestion and sleep and tears down the immune system, creating a downward spiral that can lead to an early grave. To beat cancer, it's necessary to bring stress under control. The clinic uses technology to accomplish that *fast*.

Dr. Drobot explains that the two parts of the nervous system – sympathetic and parasympathetic – may be compared to the brake and the accelerator on a car. The sympathetic nervous system is the accelerator: when you feel danger or stress, your body gets a rush of adrenaline that activates the "fight or flight" response. The parasympathetic nervous system is like the brake: when you feel relaxed and relieved, your body goes into a "rest and digest" mode. This is the mode that enables healing.

If you want to drive a car anywhere, both the brake and the accelerator need to be in good working order. But a stressed-out cancer patient's nervous system operates as if the accelerator were stuck to the floor: the sympathetic nervous system is running full bore, unable to shift into a parasympathetic "rest and digest" state for healing.

The clinic "reboots" the patient's nervous system fast

Fortunately, the clinic has machines that can "reboot" the patient's nervous system, a key step in the healing process.

Dr. Thom says, "If patients are in a revved up state, we have them lie or sit on a BioMat, an infrared device that puts people into a parasympathetic state. We have six or eight BioMats here.

"One patient was never able to go to sleep well. He did 30 minutes on a BioMat, and he was able to fall asleep immediately for the first time. BioMats are great. So many people are more sympathetic dominant than parasympathetic. The ideal is to be in a parasympathetic state *all night long*."

In addition to the BioMat, the clinic uses cryotherapy, the sound bed, and the ST-8 lymphatic machine to rebalance the nervous system.

Dr. Thom has found that "the vast majority of patients live as if they're under constant surveillance, expecting to be attacked. That's what depletes their energy. It's like turning on the furnace in the winter and leaving the front door wide open. The excess energy of a revved up nervous system is *false* energy."

Some patients need to *stop* their exercise routine!

While exercise can relieve stress, the wrong kind of exercise can impair recovery from cancer. Dr. Thom told me that some patients go to the gym and work out in the evening to burn off their excess energy. He says the gym is probably not where they should be. Instead, he suggested such alternatives as Tai Chi, Yoga, or walking the dog.

He expanded on this theme. "We more often take people off exercise than on exercise. You have to do the right exercise based on your physiology. The best exercise is still walking, no matter who you are. It moves your lymph, which allows your body to detoxify naturally. Most people don't move their lymph. They need to start *walking*."

One patient who'd been at the clinic six months earlier was in the habit of going to the gym for vigorous exercise to build up her muscles. Dr. Thom took her off that routine during her recovery. After she got better, she obtained his approval to resume her routine at the gym.

Taffy the service dog brings joy to patients

During my tour I noticed a dog in the clinic. Her name is Taffy, and she belongs to Dr. Thom. Taffy is an adorable Pomeranian. She's also a trained service dog. She loves to play with patients and delights when patients pick her up and pet her. Some patients say, "Let me pet Taffy while I'm getting my IV." This boosts their spirits.

The "Taffy effect" may be one reason why the patients do so well at this clinic. Playing with a pet at home, walking a dog, or having a purring cat on your lap also helps the healing process.

The doctors' formula for health: Obey natural laws and *have fun*!

Dr. Thom and Dr. Drobot wrote a 50-page ebook, *The Basic Treatment Guidelines*, which describes the important things they believe everyone should do. They call them natural laws. For example, every day you have to eat, chew your food, drink water, sleep, move, breathe, and so on. That's obvious, but what's not always so obvious is *how* you do those things.

One common violation of the natural law is to wolf down a meal without chewing the food properly. This causes digestive problems. So does eating food while in a state of stress. You should eat each meal in a relaxed state.

Dr. Thom says another common eating mistake is to eat and drink at the same time. The first thing a restaurant waiter asks you is, "Can I get you something to drink?" But Dr. Thom says that drinking while eating dilutes the digestive juices, which impairs digestion. He says it's better to drink in between meals, the way animals do. "Animals don't eat and drink at the same time. They eat, and then at another time they'll drink. They don't take a bite and a sip and a bite and a sip."

Inadequate sleep also violates the natural laws. Before electric lighting, people would go to sleep when it was dark and wake up at the light of morning. Habitually staying up into the wee hours of the morning can take a toll on one's health. Studies have shown that employees who have to work the night shift have a higher risk of cancer.

Proper breathing is another natural law, according to Dr. Thom. "People don't breathe! They breathe unconsciously." He recommends taking time to breathe consciously, taking deep breaths and exhaling slowly.

Proper breathing along with practices such as Yoga, Tai Chi, meditation, or prayer supports health. He says, "Every time you take a deep breath and puff your belly out, you move your diaphragm four centimeters, which pumps the liver and gives you a liver massage! It's such a simple thing. People ask me, 'Really? Will that help?' I tell them to just do it for a while and see."

Breaking natural laws causes chronic disease. Dr. Thom says, "We have to reinstate natural laws in our society and have fun. For thousands of patients I've seen, when I ask them, 'What do you do every day for fun?' they have to think about it!" For many cancer patients, the fun has practically gone out of their lives.

Dr. Thom says it's crucial for patients to find something they can do *every day* that's fun, something they really look forward to, even if it's only for 10 minutes. "If you can get people to do that on a regular basis, it's amazing how much better you can get them to feel." Doing something fun every day supports the parasympathetic nervous system.

Surprising facts about these doctors

Dr. Thom and Dr. Drobot are unusual doctors. They're not MDs but NDs – naturopathic doctors licensed by the State of Arizona, one of the few states that licenses NDs.

Now, if you think they aren't "real" doctors, consider these facts: NDs who have earned a degree from one of the recognized naturopathic medical schools are perhaps even better educated about medicine than the typical MD. That's why the State of Arizona regards licensed naturopaths as primary care physicians, just like medical doctors. What's more, Arizona authorizes naturopathic doctors to write prescriptions for any drug a patient may need.

When Dr. Thom's former student, Dr. Drobot, moved from Canada to Arizona to join his practice, he found it odd to have a prescription pad on his desk. In some Canadian provinces, naturopaths aren't authorized to prescribe drugs.

Dr. Thom started practicing naturopathic medicine by opening a clinic in Portland, Oregon. He was the only naturopath in town who would accept cancer patients because his colleagues were too scared to deal with these patients. They feared liability. They didn't know what to do. But Dr. Thom didn't want to turn cancer patients away. He felt an obligation to help them.

Dr. Thom says, "I don't know how to treat cancer, but I do know how to help the patient's physiology. The patient's body will do what it needs to do. Minimally, the patient will feel better, have better energy, gain weight, have a good appetite and good digestion, and a good quality of life. I can't cure cancer. Maybe the patient's body will be able to do that. The patient needs to be willing to participate in the treatment plan. The patient has to go home eventually. *What the patient does at home is just as important as what we do here*. That's our approach."

Here's another surprising fact about Dr. Thom. He has a dental degree and used to practice dentistry. Although he has let his dentistry license lapse, he knows all about dental problems and can refer patients to a dentist for any problem he spots that needs correcting. Certain dental problems, such as root canals and cavitations, can cause cancer in the breast, prostate, and elsewhere. That's because toxicity from an infected jaw can travel throughout the body.

Conventional doctors gave up on this 6-year-old girl

Dr. Thom told me a memorable story about a six-year-old cancer patient who almost died on the table when her parents first brought her to his clinic.

Starting at age three, this little girl had endured a monthly chemotherapy treatment for 36 months in a row. That's a lot of poison for a young girl to absorb. Then the conventional doctors stopped administering chemo because she seemed to be in remission. That was in April. She saw Dr. Thom in November of the same year because something was obviously wrong with her. She'd been lively. But for the last three days before seeing Dr. Thom she would just lie on the couch.

Her oncologist did a spinal tap and found that her spinal column was jam packed with cancer cells. He told her parents, "She's not going to make it." Meanwhile, the parents were hundreds of thousands of dollars in debt from the 36 chemo treatments because they had no medical insurance.

Here's how Dr. Thom described the girl's first visit: "Her parents carried her into the office, and that little girl lay on the table moaning and groaning in pain the whole time. I gave her a treatment right then and there. It was a much longer visit than normal. It lasted an hour and a half.

"I gave her some of the remedies, and she lay on the bed. Within 30 minutes she got off that bed, for whatever reason, and walked out! The parents were amazed. They immediately went to a health food store to pick up some items I'd recommended, and the little girl got out of the car and walked around the health store with them. She hadn't been standing at all in days."

I asked Dr. Thom, "What remedies did you give her?" He replied that he gave her "drainage" remedies for detoxification and also some homeopathic remedies from Belgium. He instructed the parents to continue giving her homeopathic treatments at home four times a day without fail.

The stench in the girl's room indicated her body was getting rid of poisons

What happened that night shocked the parents. The girl woke up in the middle of the night, having drenched the bed with sweat. Besides that, she had a rash all over her body. What's more, there was a horrible stench in the room, as if someone had just died in it.

The parents said it was "unbelievable." They immediately filled up the bath tub and scrubbed her down. They washed the sheets but couldn't get the smell out and had to burn them. The same thing happened three nights in a row: drenching the bed, the horrible smell, and the all-body rash.

What caused the drenched bed, the stench, and the rash? It was the poison from 36 chemo treatments coming out of the girl through detox as a result of Dr. Thom's homeopathic treatment!

This girl lived for the next ten months as a normal child at home. Her quality of life was excellent. In the 11th month she quickly went downhill and passed away peacefully, not in any pain, nausea, or misery. It's a blessing that Dr. Thom's treatment was able to give her ten bonus months with her family and friends during which she felt good. If only this girl's parents had taken her to Dr. Thom as a *first* resort instead of putting her through 36 chemo treatments, I believe she'd probably be alive today.

I asked Dr. Drobot for his theory on why the girl died after doing so well for ten months. He replied that this happened long before the clinic accumulated the impressive array of machines and therapies they have now. Dr. Thom treated this girl with what he had available at the time: homeopathic remedies and nutrition. These remedies produced dramatic results, considering that the girl already had one foot in the grave when he first saw her. But such remedies can only go so far. That's why

Dr. Thom and Dr. Drobot have accumulated such an impressive collection of powerful therapeutic machines.

Dr. Drobot also mentioned that some of his cancer patients choose to do both conventional therapy *and* natural therapy. He told me this often works quite well, adding that oncologists ask the clinic what the patients are doing. The oncologists are amazed that the patients do so well before and after chemotherapy, unlike their other chemo patients who are just plain miserable and weak. The radiologists, too, are amazed that patients who do natural therapies don't get radiation burns, unlike their other patients.

If a patient is bent on having chemotherapy and radiation, there *can* be a good outcome if the patient also plugs into a clinic like the American Center for Biological Medicine. As for those who've already done chemo and radiation *alone* without any natural therapy, they desperately need alternative therapies to rebuild, to the extent possible, what the toxic therapies have destroyed.

This hardcore skeptic got a big bonus

Dr. Thom told me another memorable story about a 65-year-old veterinarian who went through hell during conventional treatment for esophageal cancer. A surgeon removed the patient's esophagus and pulled his stomach into his throat. Other doctors gave him the standard radiation and chemo. But he was obviously in a downward spiral leading to the grave. Finally, the doctors gave him the grim prognosis: "You're done. Get your affairs in order."

When he appeared in Dr. Thom's office, he was in terrible shape with one foot in the grave and an unhelpful attitude. Dr. Thom asked him, "Why are you here?" He replied, "My wife made me come. I don't believe in anything you do. I don't believe in alternative medicine. I have no other choice. I've given up because the doctors told me nothing could be done. My wife heard about you and said maybe you have something to offer."

Dr. Thom replied, "I believe I do, but I need you at least to participate. You have to do the work. You have to do what I tell you to do."

The man didn't have time to answer before his wife answered for him. She said, "He's going to be doing exactly what you say! Don't worry." His wife made sure he followed Dr. Thom's instructions *to the letter*. The man was astonished to find himself getting better. His health improved so much that he resumed his normal activities.

A year and a half later – it was in June – the man told Dr. Thom, "I used to go fishing in Alaska every year with my sons. I'd like to go with them this year. Can I go?" Dr. Thom answered, "Yes, I think you're in a good place to go." So he went fishing again in Alaska with his sons and had a fabulous time. Upon returning, he gave Dr. Thom a few big salmon as a token of gratitude. That was in July.

The man returned to the clinic in August because he didn't feel right. Dr. Thom asked him, "What's going on?" He said, "I didn't want to tell you in June, but I sensed that something was sort of off." He died that October. But during his 20 bonus months he saw three grandchildren born, went to graduations of nieces and nephews, and attended a family wedding, in addition to the memorable fishing trip in Alaska with his sons – *without feeling miserable.*

Dr. Thom told me, "When you see a case like that, you know you're really helping people." This case, too, happened before the clinic accumulated its array of powerful therapeutic machines.

Businessman narrowly avoids getting a feeding tube for life

Dr. Drobot told me about a wealthy Canadian businessman who had a horrendous cancer of the throat in 2006. He did undergo surgery for it, a decision that Dr. Drobot said was a good idea. But then his doctor recommended jaw radiation – a drastic treatment that would've destroyed the man's ability to eat! He hated the idea of being fed through a tube for the rest of his life.

Normally he would've been skeptical of natural medicine, but, out of desperation, he came to Dr. Drobot and was open to natural therapies.

Dr. Drobot said, "He's still with us today, has been cancer free for over five years, and is doing just fine. He's as pleased as punch to be able to eat and live normally." The man had met two people with the same kind of cancer he had. Each of them opted for the jaw radiation, as the oncologist recommended. Those two men are now six feet under the sod.

Oncologists wonder how this man can be cancer free

Two years ago an Arizona man in his late 60s straggled into the clinic. He suffered from lymphoma and had followed his conventional doctor's recommendation to have chemotherapy. But just one round of the chemo had almost killed him. In Dr. Drobot's clinic, this man went through the immune-boosting protocols and the machine therapies and became free of cancer – an outcome the oncologists can't understand!

For this man, chemo was "it" – the only therapy the oncologists could offer. Once it became clear he couldn't tolerate it, they had *nothing* to offer. Fortunately, he found his way to a clinic that offers hope.

Lyme disease? No problem!

Lyme disease has baffled conventional doctors ever since it was first identified and described in 1975. All they know how to do is throw industrial-strength antibiotics at it and hope for the best.

Conventional doctors claim that antibiotics work *if* the disease is correctly diagnosed and *if* it's treated early enough. Otherwise, patients can spin their wheels for years taking round after round of heavy-duty antibiotics to no avail. To make things even worse, overuse of antibiotics causes other health problems.

One desperate Lyme disease sufferer came to the American Center for Biological Medicine as a last resort. Incredibly, he'd been taking antibiotics for his Lyme disease for 16 years. Dr. Thom posed the question: "At what point does someone say, 'The treatment isn't working'?"

I asked Dr. Thom why Lyme disease has become such a problem. He replied, "If you line up 150 people who got bitten by a deer tick, they won't all get Lyme disease. Why not? Because their bio-terrain – the milieu within their bodies – is different. That's what we treat.

"Usually when someone has Lyme disease there's a defect in their detoxification. When they got bitten by the tick, their health was already weakened. People who are detoxing normally can easily get rid of the Lyme spirochete."

Dr. Thom and Dr. Drobot never use antibiotics for Lyme disease, although they're authorized to prescribe them. The clinic's natural treatments are effective at getting rid of Lyme disease for good, and they improve the patient's overall health to boot.

Are headaches caused by an Excedrin deficiency?

Patients come to the clinic with a wide variety of health problems – not just cancer. One patient had been suffering from severe headaches. Dr. Thom asked her, "What do you do for headache relief?" She replied, "I take Excedrin." He replied, "Are your headaches caused by an Excedrin deficiency?" She got the point. Diagnostic testing enabled Dr. Thom to get to the bottom of what was causing her headaches so he could remedy the problem.

Whether someone has a headache or cancer, it's necessary to treat the cause instead of masking the symptom while ignoring the cause.

Patients get the best of both worlds

Patients at the American Center for Biological Medicine don't see just one of the doctors. They see both Dr. Thom and Dr. Drobot, who have a vast amount of experience between them. Each doctor has his own style, and getting the complementary insights of both doctors gives patients the best of both worlds.

The cost of treatment at the American Center for Biological Medicine depends on the type and severity of the cancer. It costs pennies on the dollar compared to conventional treatment. It's an outpatient clinic, and the staff there can advise you about affordable options for lodging near the clinic.

Dr. Drobot also practices medicine for one

week each month in Calgary, Alberta. His contact information at the Canadian clinic follows below.

Contact information for the Scottsdale, Arizona, clinic:

Dr. Dickson Thom, D.D.S., N.D.
Dr. Jeoff Drobot, N.M.D.
The American Center for Biological Medicine
9312 E. Raintree Drive
Scottsdale, AZ 85260
Phone: 480-614-5820
Website: www.TheBioMedCenter.com

Contact information for Dr. Drobot's Calgary, Alberta, clinic:

Dr. Jeoff Drobot, N.M.D.
The Calgary Centre for Naturopathic Medicine
6620 Crowchild Trail SW
Calgary, Alberta
Canada T3E 5R8
Phone: 403-270-9355
Website: www.CalgaryNaturopathic.com

Chapter Three

The young doctor with perhaps the world's best documented success in cancer treatment

Dr. Colleen Huber, N.M.D., of Tempe, Arizona, makes a bold claim on her website. She declares, "We have the best results of any cancer clinic we can find in the world: 85 percent success for the people completing our treatments."

This record of success includes all of her cancer patients from Stage One through Stage Four. Dr. Huber doesn't "cherry pick" patients to make her statistics look better. She never turns away a patient for being too sick. She explains, "We exclude no one. All are welcome. And we report the data for all patients, our successes as well as our failures. If you consider our Stage One through early Stage Four patients, our success rate is 92 percent. (Not so good with late Stage Four). No other cancer clinic in the world of any kind has such a high success rate."

Those results are spectacular!

Dr. Huber states on her website: "If you find a clinic with better results, we want to know about it!"

Although I know of no clinic with *better* documented results, it's worth mentioning that Dr. James Forsythe, M.D., is in the midst of a five-year study of 500 Stage Four cancer patients who sought treatment at his clinic. His results so far are impressive.

Comparing Dr. Forsythe's statistics with Dr. Huber's is like comparing apples and oranges. That's because Dr. Huber's statistics include all stages of cancer, while the 500 cancer patients in Dr. Forsythe's study are all Stage Four. See chapter four about Dr. James Forsythe, "The Doctor Who Cures the 'Incurables'", for information about his groundbreaking study.

I arrived early for my appointment to interview Dr. Huber at her clinic, so the receptionist gave me a tour. She told me that nine patients out of 10 are there for cancer treatment. The clinic has a Kangan water machine to alkalize water, and patients help themselves to this water and take some with them when they leave.

The receptionist told me that some patients have had success obtaining reimbursement from their health insurance company: "United Health Care and Aetna pay pretty well if the deductible has been met. Patients with those companies get about half. Blue Cross doesn't pay for anything. They'll pay a million dollars for cut-burn-poison, but they won't pay $20,000 for natural treatments here."

When Dr. Huber sat down at her desk for the interview, I asked her if I could turn on my digital audio recorder, which I call my "harmonica" because it's about the size of a small harmonica. I told her that I record interviews because I don't want to miss anything, and I can't write or type as fast as the recorder can capture words. She asked me to hold off on taping until she clearly understood my purpose. I explained that I only wanted information about her clinic to present to my readers. When she realized I wasn't looking for kickbacks or referral bonuses but only for information, she gave me the OK to turn on my recorder.

I asked Dr. Huber to tell me her story. She explained that she became interested in natural medicine at an early age because her father was a fan of homeopathy, organic food, gardening, and healthy living.

Her interest intensified when she learned that the well-known Sloan-Kettering Cancer Center fired Dr. Ralph Moss for blowing the whistle on them. Sloan-Kettering had sponsored research showing that laetrile kills cancer cells, but they instructed Dr. Moss to lie about the research results. Her father commented, "Laetrile is from apricot seeds. How can that be made illegal? It shrinks tumors."

While she was still a teenager she told her father she wanted to go to medical school. He said no, and that was the end of the discussion. So she became a Spanish and Italian translator and lived in Latin America for a while. Later, she went to osteopathic school, but the school's emphasis on drugs, drugs, drugs turned her off. She wanted to practice *natural* medicine, so she transferred to the Southwest College of Naturopathic Medicine, which she told me is much tougher than medical school with twice as many courses required.

Dr. Huber declared, "We have a saying at this clinic: 'Cancer doesn't take a vacation.' So it's tough for me to take a vacation. When I opened this clinic in 2006 my goal was to provide cancer treatment." She built her practice from scratch – an impressive achievement.

She said her clinic once employed a promising intern. But the intern went to a residency at the Cancer Treatment Centers of America (CTCA), which required her to knuckle under, compromise her principles, and accept its preference for chemotherapy and radiation.

"I've seen about 400 patients," Dr. Huber said, "and I work with them in depth, three times a week for 30 minutes at a time. You get to know them well and watch the progress. We have other advantages over places like CTCA. Most cancer clinics have to watch people become sicker, and we get to watch people become healthier. Granted, some people here get sicker, but most people get better."

"Pancreatic cancer is one of the easier cancers"

In the IV room, the receptionist had introduced me to a pancreatic cancer patient named John. When I mentioned to Dr. Huber that pancreatic cancer is a tough one, she replied, "It's not that pancreatic cancer is so difficult. It's that chemo doesn't work on it. For us, pancreatic cancer is one of the easier cancers when it hasn't yet spread."

I was shocked. Pancreatic is one of the easier cancers? I'd never before heard that in my life. I found it hard to believe, but after I interviewed John I became convinced that Dr. Huber actually *can* handle pancreatic cancer.

John told me his story as I sat next to him in the IV room. Ten months earlier he had started turning yellow. Bile was blocked from entering his intestine, as it should, and his stool was snow white. He was referred to a specialist who inserted a tube to open up his bile duct and, in the process, discovered pancreatic cancer.

Conventional doctors told him he had "three months to live." But when I interviewed him ten months later, he was still very much alive and kicking.

As John put it, "The doctor who told me I had three months to live didn't lie. He had the statistics to back him up." This doctor explained that John's cancer was too advanced for surgery and that he should "go home and get your affairs in order. When the time comes, I'll put you in hospice, give you drugs to control the pain, and you'll fade away and die."

John had no reason to doubt his doctor and considered himself under a death sentence. One of his neighbors had died of pancreatic cancer. She had lasted three months, spending her last month as a "vegetable." John figured that would be his fate, too.

But events took a different turn.

One of John's relatives had come to Dr. Huber's clinic for his colon cancer and was so happy with the treatment, he suggested that John see Dr. Huber, too. So John flew to Arizona, had three IVs at Dr. Huber's clinic, and then flew back home to Utah for a week, during which he had more tests. His Utah doctors told him – again – that he was done for. They gave him no hope that the IV treatments in Arizona would help him.

John told me, "I figured, well, I'm done now. I'll just live it out and die. So my wife and I moved down here to Arizona. My wife works for Walmart, and she transferred her employment to a Walmart down here." Though John started out with an attitude of hopelessness about his cancer, somehow Dr. Huber gave him confidence that he could get rid of his cancer at her clinic.

Dying patient regains health, plans a trip to New Zealand!

These days, said John, "I come in here two times a week for IVs, and I literally am feeling fantastic. I feel I'm here on false pretenses. I'm starting new businesses and doing everything I can. I'm going to Australia and New Zealand – I'm from New Zealand originally." John is confident that his future is as bright as the Arizona sunshine.

I asked John if he would recommend this clinic to someone else who has cancer. He replied, "Oh, absolutely. This place is amazing. I wish they could treat people in other parts of the country and the world. This treatment is just not available in other parts. I'm glad I found Dr. Huber and am doing this. It's worked out *really* well."

John said another benefit of the clinic is its affordability: "The clinic charges only a nominal fee compared to the cost of taking IVs in the hospital. And yet the insurance company won't pay for it. I've been going at it full time for eight months, and I've spent about $15,000. If I'm here for IVs three times a week, it's $810 a week, so it's about $3,000 a month. That has dropped off because I only come in twice a week now."

Dr. Huber drives the oldest car in the parking lot

Concerning costs, Dr. Huber says, "I have a razor thin profit margin. I'm still driving the oldest car in the parking lot, but that's fine. I don't want to skimp on the ingredients in the IV. They ARE the finest that money can buy. We charge $270 per IV. If the patient gets three IVs a week, that's $810 a week.

"Ideally, patients should stay for six months of treatment. But if it's an uncomplicated cancer, such as breast cancer, and if a lumpectomy had clean margins without metastasis, three months is enough. The worst cancers need six months. When the cancer seems to have gone into remission, it's wise to continue treatment for *another* three months. It's not unheard of for people to be here a year or more, and it's certainly a pleasant place to spend a few months."

The $810 weekly cost of Dr. Huber's treatment is incredibly low! Dr. Huber told me, "I don't want to treat a cancer patient for only three or four weeks. Three or four weeks of treatment sets the cancer back a little bit, but we're not finished yet! You have to keep fighting cancer longer than you think you have to."

Another patient I met in the IV room was Jim, who also told me the story of his struggle with prostate cancer. Ten years ago, when his PSA became elevated, his doctor wanted to perform a biopsy (cutting out small tissue samples to be analyzed for cancer cells). Jim said no. He'd been operated on a couple of times, but he'd promised himself he'd never do that again.

He doesn't trust the medical profession, the FDA, the AMA, or the drug companies. As he puts it, "The whole system is corrupt, and I don't want anything to do with it. I don't want to go near it. I found this clinic through my research. This clinic is fabulous. The people are great."

Jim's "thousand-dollar-a-week habit"

The only problem is that Jim's insurance company won't cover the treatment. He says, "I laughingly call it my thousand-dollar-a-week habit. I was here for 12 weeks. $12,000 for 12 weeks isn't bad. But I ran out of money and had to quit. I changed my financial situation significantly, came back, and I've been at this for the last eight weeks. Now I'm doing the IVs three times a week at $270 a pop. That's $810 a week.

"Dr. Huber has had tremendous success with prostate cancer. I have absolutely no symptoms. Her treatment has worked for 128 others, so I'm going to be number 129. If you go to the clinic's website, Dr. Huber lists all of her patients without mentioning their names. She lists what stage they were when they arrived, the kind of cancer, and what the percentage of cure is for each different category of cancer. It's very unique. Very complete. If you arrive here at Stage One and go through the treatments, you're going to leave here cured – virtually 100 percent.

"A lady named Carline came down here with a brain tumor behind her left eye. It'd screwed her eye up. She'd gone through some radiation, but they couldn't operate on her cancer. She came down here for about a year and walked out cured."

Pointing to John, Jim said, "They told this guy, 'John, you're dead.' And sometimes he acts dead." John laughed.

Dr. Huber told me that John's doctors in Utah had brainwashed him that he was going to die in three months. She said, "When he first came to me he told me, 'Look, I know I have only a couple of months left. After I die, my wife will go back to Utah.' I said, 'Wait a minute. You're not in a wheelchair. You have no organ damage. Stage One through early Stage Four is a hopeful category – a category we can probably help.'"

Even in cases of late Stage Four cancer – those cases in which the cancer has spread far from its original site – Dr. Huber can offer a better quality of life and some increase in quantity. She has been able to send some late Stage Four cancers into remission, but these cases are difficult.

Although some patients come to her clinic when it's too late, Dr. Huber tells the patients, "Avoid thoughts that begin with 'coulda, woulda, shoulda.' Today is day one. Let's move forward. Let's see what we can do and where we can go from here.

"There's another therapeutic thing we do here. We have the chairs in the IV room in a circle because the spontaneous support group they form with each other is priceless. It has therapeutic value. A new patient comes into the room for his IV and looks around and thinks to himself, 'Well, you don't look too bad, and you don't look too bad, and all of you look better than the people I saw going through chemotherapy. Maybe my doctor was wrong when he told me I had one or two months to live because here's someone who was given three months and that was a couple of years ago.' The new patient's pessimism turns into optimism."

A simple key to Dr. Huber's success

Dr. Huber said, "An important thing we do here – a key to success – is getting patients not to eat sugar! Sugar feeds cancer. They really have to stay away from it."

Dr. Huber is proud of how well her patients are doing. She said, "Jim is 70, and he bench presses 200 pounds. Another cancer patient climbed the highest mountain in Arizona a few months ago. Three cancer patients hiked the Grand Canyon from the top to the bottom and back up – not an easy hike!"

Where to stay when you're a patient of Dr. Huber

Dr. Huber's clinic has lodging arrangements with three apartment complexes within a square mile. These are studio apartments. There's a Whole Foods store nearby.

Contact information:

Dr. Colleen Huber, N.M.D.
Nature Works Best
1250 E. Baseline Rd., Suite 205
Tempe, AZ 85283
Phone: 480-839-2800
Website: www.NatureWorksBest.com
Email: office@NatureWorksBest.com

Chapter Four

The doctor who cures the "incurables"

"We've seen patients go into full remission with aggressive, Stage Four cancers, and we see continued positive responses in others with chemo-resistant cancer."

~ Dr. James Forsythe, M.D.

Seventeen-year-old Valerie M. from Texas was pretty much on her deathbed in 2004, according to James Forsythe, M.D., H.M.D., when her family brought her to his cancer clinic in Reno, Nevada. She had Ewing's sarcoma, a deadly cancer that arises in bones.

Valerie had been treated with conventional cancer therapies at the finest cancer hospitals in Texas, but to no avail. Her doctors gave up on her. They told her to go home and get her affairs in order because – according to them "nothing more can be done."

As her cancer spread, both of Valerie's lungs developed large nodules. And there was a big hole in the left side of her pelvis. She was nearly unable to walk. Her left leg was swollen. She was in a great deal of pain.

Dr. Forsythe offered Valerie's family hope and said he'd do his best to reverse her cancer.

After just two weeks of alternative cancer therapy, Valerie could walk around without difficulty. By the time she got home, her lesions of the lung had disappeared. Her doctors in Texas were flabbergasted.

Valerie's astonishing and seemingly miraculous cure was featured in a video called "The Incurables."

How did Dr. Forsythe cure this "incurable" 17-year-old? He used three main therapies:

- A patented natural food supplement called Poly-MVA. Poly-MVA is a highly regarded cancer remedy. It's featured in one of our Special Reports, *Natural Cancer Remedies that Work*. (See www.naturalcancerremedies.com.)
- A series of intravenous treatments known as Forsythe Immune Therapy.
- A regimen of low-dose chemotherapy. Unlike conventional full-dose chemo, which hits the patient like a sledgehammer, Dr. Forsythe's low-dose regimen doesn't cause side effects such as nausea, hair loss, or low energy, nor does it destroy the patient's immune system.

Dr. Forsythe is a rare bird among oncologists: He's "double-boarded"

You may wonder how a medical doctor specializing in oncology can use homeopathic treatments. After all, you'd think that an oncologist is limited to such treatments as surgery, radiation, and chemo.

The answer might surprise you: Dr. Forsythe is perhaps the only physician in America who's a board-certified oncologist *and* a board-certified doctor of homeopathy. In other words, he's "double-boarded." This gives him the qualifications and the freedom to push the envelope by using conventional medicine or natural medicine or both at once. As he did in Valerie's case, Dr. Forsythe often uses both. This is what's meant by "integrative medicine" – sometimes called "the best of both worlds."

It's often taken for granted that everyone chooses conventional treatment before homeopathic treatment, but that's not the case. The Queen of England, for example, can afford any kind of medical treatment she wants. But when she gets sick she sees a homeopath rather than a conventional doctor.

A study is underway to prove his method beats conventional treatment

As sensational as Valerie's cure was, Dr. Forsythe knows that many conventional doctors would just shrug off her case. Some would say, "She was lucky." Others would say, "It's a case of spontaneous remission," which is just a fancy way of saying the same thing.

I asked Dr. Forsythe a question I've wrestled with. What's the answer to someone who asks, "Why hasn't my doctor heard about this supposedly great cure?"

Dr. Forsythe replied, "It's necessary to have large numbers of patients and good clinical studies that are well controlled. And then you present your data and go head to head with the data in conventional oncology's own literature. We can beat their two percent five-year survival rate, and that's what I intend to do with my current study."

You may be wondering exactly what this "two percent five-year survival rate" means. He's referring to the five-year survival rate for late-stage cancer patients who choose conventional treatments like chemotherapy. It's well-established the survival rate of such patients is around two percent.

This means if you take 100 cases of tough, Stage Four cancers — the kind of cancers usually considered incurable – and treat them with conventional chemotherapy, radiation and surgery, only two will still be alive five years later.

That's right: Just two patients out of 100. This is not only a terrible result, but the other 98 die in sheer misery — with vomiting, fatigue, hair loss, and nausea. The treatments are so awful, many patients refuse them even though their doctors falsely promise the treatments will extend their lives.

Dr. Forsythe is in the midst of a five-year study of 500 Stage Four cancer patients. As this is written in 2013, he's three years into this study, which will take seven more years to complete. So far, he has 450 of the 500 Stage Four cancer patients he needs for the study. Eventually, he'll have the sample size of 500 he needs. Dr. Forsythe's study will monitor each of the 500 patients five years from the start of treatment.

Even at this early stage in the study, Dr. Forsythe's results beat the results of conventional cancer doctors by a country mile. Here are the *two-year* results for Stage Four breast cancer patients after the start of treatment:

- National Cancer Institute (NCI) study based on conventional cancer treatment: 44 patients out of 100 were still alive after two years.
- Cancer Treatment Centers of America (CTCA) study based on CTCA's conventional cancer treatment with some natural therapies added: 63 patients out of 100 were still alive after two years.
- Dr. Forsythe's study based on his own patients: 85 patients out of 100 were still alive after two years.

As you can see, Dr. Forsythe's two-year results far surpass the results reported by CTCA and the NCI. It bears repeating that the NCI's five-year results for conventional treatment are miserable: just two patients out of 100 are still alive. Even though Dr. Forsythe is only three years into his study, which will take another seven years to complete, it's already obvious that his five-year results will outperform those of conventional cancer treatment.

Unlike some establishment cancer researchers, Dr. Forsythe doesn't cherry-pick the patients for his 500-patient study. Many of them, like Valerie, were practically at death's door when they came to his clinic as a last hope.

In Dr. Forsythe's 500-patient study, he doesn't include Stage Four cancer patients who die within the first month of treatment. That's because it was too late for *any* kind of treatment to extend the lives of these patients.

He includes in his study patients who make it

past the first month. And even if a patient dies of something other than cancer, such as a heart attack, within five years after starting treatment, Dr. Forsythe counts the death as a cancer death for the purpose of the study. That's because he doesn't want to give conventional doctors any excuse or pretext to reject his study.

Conventional doctors will have to accept that his treatments outperform theirs – or deny the plain truth.

As an added bonus, Dr. Forsythe's methods have almost no adverse side effects. Compare that to the well-known, miserable side effects of conventional high-dose chemotherapy – which are all for nothing, as the patients die anyway. The most that conventional medicine can claim for late-stage cancer treatments is that they extend a patient's life by a few weeks or months – and even that is doubtful.

Dr. Forsythe's approach wins hands down! It's a "no brainer."

Not only does Dr. Forsythe have an abundance of "anecdotal" success stories of turning around the most difficult Stage Four, "incurable" cancers. But he also has the statistical proof to back up the anecdotes and he's gathering more evidence every day.

You'd think the American cancer establishment would beat a path to Dr. Forsythe's door to ask him, "How are you curing those Stage Four cancers that we haven't been able to cure?"

Keep in mind the historical context of Dr. Forsythe's cancer breakthrough.

In 1971 President Richard Nixon responded to America's cancer crisis by declaring a "War on Cancer." This "war" was supposed to be similar in scope to President John F. Kennedy's challenge to put a man on the moon within 10 years.

Since the start of the "War on Cancer" in1971, the American cancer industry has spent literally *billions* of dollars, supposedly on trying to find better treatments and even a cure for cancer.

After all those years and all those billions of dollars spent, what have the cancer researchers come up with? All they have is the same old surgery/radiation/chemotherapy they had back in 1971! And this cut/burn/poison regimen still offers only a two percent success rate for patients with advanced cancer.

For the American cancer industry, nothing has really changed since 1971! They've accomplished practically nothing.

The federal government beats a path to Dr. Forsythe's door

Dr. Forsythe's success rate is remarkable, especially when you compare it to that of the cancer industry. The federal government did beat a path to Dr. Forsythe's door over his discovery, but not for the reasons you'd expect.

One February morning in 2005, Dr. Forsythe was enjoying breakfast at home with his wife in Reno, Nevada. The American flag was proudly waving in the breeze from his front yard flagpole.

But then his wife noticed something odd through the window.

Three black sport utility vehicles pulled up the driveway. Out came three groups of agents bearing three different insignias on their flak jackets: four agents were from the FBI, four were from the FDA, and four were from the ICE (Immigration Customs Enforcement).

Mrs. Forsythe asked her husband, "What are those people doing on the driveway?"

He replied, "I don't know. I'll go see."

Dr. Forsythe opened the door just in the nick of time because an agent with a "door buster" was on the verge of smashing his door open.

The 12 agents had their guns drawn and pointed them at Dr. Forsythe.

Aghast with amazement, he asked, "Is this a joke?"

An agent replied, "We have a search warrant for your home and your business."

Rogue agent holds gun to Dr. Forsythe's head

The agents pushed him into the room and made him kneel down. Holding a gun to his head, they searched him. They asked, "Who else is in the house?" He replied, "Just my wife."

At about that time, Mrs. Forsythe came down the hallway. She had heard the commotion. The agents also held a gun to her chest and frisked her. She said later that it was like being raped.

Then the agents marched both of them into the house and separated them. They were under custody in their own home — but without having been read their Miranda rights.

Agents searched the house for seven hours, rifling every drawer and taking boxes and boxes of files, financial records, credit card records, and every computer in the house. They found nothing incriminating because there was nothing to find.

You see, Dr. Forsythe is a patriotic, law-abiding American. He had done nothing wrong. His patients love him. He's never been the target of a malpractice lawsuit in his entire career.

At the same time this home invasion was in progress, other agents were zooming in on Dr. Forsythe's clinic. They told the patients, "You should go home because Dr. Forsythe is involved in criminal activity."

The agents asked the patients if they could take their confidential medical charts. All the patients said no. But the agents took them anyway — in brazen defiance of doctor-patient confidentiality!

The agents separated Dr. Forsythe's staff members to interrogate them, in violation of their Miranda rights. The agents told each staff member, "Dr. Forsythe is engaged in criminal activity. Are you sure you want to work here? Do you know you could be in jeopardy yourself ?"

Despite the intense pressure and intimidation, Dr. Forsythe's staff didn't quit. He was able to keep his clinic open during the time of severe persecution.

Dr. Forsythe arrested, fingerprinted, strip-searched

Finally, in September of 2006 Dr. Forsythe was formally arrested — supposedly for irregularities in prescribing drugs. The authorities pounded on his door during business hours. They took him to police headquarters for a mug shot, fingerprinting, and a strip search.

The jury's unanimous verdict: NOT GUILTY!

At his first court appearance, the magistrate asked Dr. Forsythe, "How do you plead?" He replied, "Not guilty, your Honor. I haven't done anything wrong."

And the jury concluded the same thing after Dr. Forsythe's trial, which the Las Vegas press labeled "the trial of the century." On November 1, 2007, after only one hour of deliberation, the jury announced its unanimous verdict: "not guilty."

The "not guilty" verdict gave Dr. Forsythe his reputation back. He still has his medical license, his clinic, and his staff. He's open for business and eager to help more patients overcome cancer.

And the "not guilty" verdict was a terrible setback for the mainstream, conventional American cancer industry.

Why did the federal government beat a path to Dr. Forsythe's door to harass him instead of heralding him as a hero for his cancer breakthroughs? Sadly, the answer is that too much money is at stake for the cancer industry to lightly give it up.

The typical cost of treating a cancer patient with the standard treatments — surgery, radiation, and chemo — can climb as high as $850,000. But if Dr. Forsythe helps that patient get rid of his cancer with inexpensive alternative treatments, the conventional cancer doctors will be out all that revenue.

Perhaps major drug companies and conventional cancer doctors believe Dr. Forsythe is eating their lunch. But if they're sincere, how could they possibly want to get rich from using outmoded, ineffective treatments that needlessly cause pain and usually result in death?

Perhaps mainstream medicine should take a closer look at Dr. Forsythe's alternative treatments such as Poly-MVA and Forsythe Immune Therapy.

How Poly-MVA makes cancer cells fizzle out

As mentioned earlier, Poly-MVA is a patented food supplement. Here's how it works, in Dr. Forsythe's own words:

"Cancer cells are anaerobic. In other words, they require very little oxygen to function and reproduce. They thrive on simple sugars. They also like low-oxygen environments for their metabolism.

"Poly-MVA consists of palladium, lipoic acid, B12, and thiamine. This combination of ingredients is natural and nontoxic. It interferes with the metabolism of the cancer cell. When administered to advanced cancer patients, Poly-MVA appears to have the unique capacity to negatively affect anaerobic cells while supporting healthy tissues. Simply put, this nutrient attacks the 'engine room' of a cancer cell, short circuiting the cell's energy production, thereby destroying it."

Dr. Forsythe says that Poly-MVA is most effective on breast cancer, prostate cancer, and non-small-cell lung cancer. His other key therapy, Forsythe Immune Therapy, has demonstrated success with *all* kinds of cancers.

Forsythe Immune Therapy includes a proprietary blend of vitamins, minerals, and natural substances that boost the immune system.

Dr. Forsythe's other therapies and recommendations

Conventional medicine rejects the idea, but research suggests that dental problems can cause cancer — even in locations far from the mouth. Dr. Forsythe accepts this finding and uses it successfully to treat cancer patients.

For example, a root canal can sometimes lead to an infection in the jawbone. Dr. Forsythe contends that the infection can spread, causing breast cancer, prostate cancer, and other cancers.

It does little good to treat cancer if you ignore its underlying cause. That's why Dr. Forsythe works with a biological dentist. A biological dentist is an alternative dentist who avoids the use of mercury amalgam fillings and root canals.

The biological dentist who works with Dr. Forsythe gives each of his cancer patients a dental evaluation to determine whether a dental problem may be causing the cancer. If so, the dentist fixes the problem.

Detoxification is another key strategy

Dr. Forsythe strongly believes in detoxification for cancer patients. That's because reducing the body's toxic load helps the healing process.

He recommends several methods to detoxify the body, including chelation therapy, colonic hydrotherapy, and far infrared saunas. He doesn't offer all of these services at his clinic; some of them are available offsite.

As you may know, colonic hydrotherapy irrigates the colon with four or five gallons of water in a process that takes about an hour. This is perhaps the best method of dislodging the fecal matter that can accumulate in the colon. Many of the top alternative cancer doctors advocate colonic hydrotherapy.

Concerning diet, Dr. Forsythe recommends that his cancer patients consume large amounts of the three Bs and the three Cs. The three Bs are beans, broccoli, and Brussels sprouts. The three Cs are carrots, cauliflower, and cabbage.

He also recommends "green powders" (wheatgrass, rye, barley, and algae powders), which help alkalize the body. (Cancer cells thrive in an acidic environment.) Dr. Forsythe recommends powders manufactured by a company called Boku.

To help his patients alkalize their bodies, Dr. Forsythe also wants them to drink a gallon of alkalized water a day. Each day, patients bring in their empty water jugs and fill them up from the clinic's alkaline water dispenser.

Dr. Forsythe recommends that his patients buy an Athena or Kangan alkalizing water machine for home use. If a patient can't afford one of these machines, Dr. Forsythe suggests the patient can take a teaspoon of baking soda in four ounces of water at least two or three times a day. Another option he mentioned is Alka Seltzer Gold, which is bicarbonate and aspirin. This will raise the body's pH.

Dr. Forsythe advises patients to avoid sugar, whole milk products, fried foods, red meats, cured meats, and anything else that's cured. He encourages patients to drink such juices as noni, mangosteen, and acai.

Dr. Forsythe's secret weapon: The Greek cancer test

Dr. Forsythe attributes much of his success to the blood test for each cancer patient that he sends to a lab in Greece for analysis. "With the Greek test," he explained, "you don't need a tumor sample. It's hard to get a chunk of tumor for a test. The Greek test is done on cancer cells in circulating blood. Through high tech means, the Greek lab isolates cancer cells and breaks them down genetically.

"When they're finished, they're able to tell which 21 agents will work best on the patient's particular cancer. We don't want to use something that's only 20 or 30 percent successful. We want something that's 80 percent effective or higher. When we show the patient the results of the Greek test, it gives the patient an enormous amount of confidence that the treatment is going to work!

"Before we had the Greek test, I would have to *guess* which drugs might work. It's no longer a guessing game. Whenever a doctor gives a patient chemo that *doesn't* work, he's giving the patient a poison, injuring the immune system, delaying the appropriate treatment, allowing the cancer to grow, putting the patient even further behind the eight ball, and causing the patient to die sooner.

"Low dose chemo works well when you *know* what will work well based on the Greek test."

Showing me one example of the test's results, Dr. Forsythe said, "In this particular patient, the test identified 22 agents that would work best. Therefore, the patient knows he's getting the best drugs.

"The test also shows what supplements work best – the natural remedies. So instead of giving the patient 50 or 60 supplements, I give the patient 10 or 12 of the best supplements. That becomes their daily supply.

"In some cases, we give our patients the best hormones as well. So we've got three things going for us: the best drugs, the best supplements, and the best hormones. This is the blueprint for their remission. It's remarkable. I can explain it to you in a short time, and you get it. But conventional oncologists don't want to hear about it."

Case Study: Doctors tell Bernadette, "Nothing can be done for your brain tumor"

Bernadette's life changed the day she was hit by a drunken driver. Within two years of her injury, the pain in her head became excruciating.

Her doctors in New York gave her an MRI, a CAT scan, and other tests. They found nothing. So they told her she had a psychological disorder. They said she was "inventing" her pain.

Every morning at 4:30 a.m. Bernadette started taking the painkillers necessary to start her day. She said the pain felt like a rake with a million sharp prongs scraping through her brain. She also suffered double vision and had to get special glasses so she could see normally.

After she had endured years of suffering, doctors gave Bernadette another MRI that revealed a brain tumor! She felt vindicated. She knew her pain had always been real and not a psychological invention, and now she knew the cause of it.

But her doctors told her, "There's nothing we can do for you. Chemo and radiation won't help. And the tumor is inoperable. Go home and we'll make sure you're comfortable."

She asked, "How are you going to make me comfortable?" They replied, "We'll give you pain killers." She responded, "I don't want painkillers. I don't want to live on painkillers."

In fact, Bernadette's tumor had appeared on a

CAT scan four years earlier, but her doctors had missed it.

Bernadette now says, "I'm ready to take on the world!"

Because Bernadette's New York doctors could do nothing for her, she decided to give Dr. Forsythe's program at the Century Wellness Clinic a try. After just a week of treatment, she says, "I didn't need my glasses anymore. I had worn them for six years. That was a miracle!" After two more weeks of treatment, she went home.

Her headaches were gone. Her pain was gone. Her tumor was gone, as proved by a new MRI. Bernadette says, "What can I say? This is amazing. I had been written off by doctors who said, 'Make sure your will is signed.' But now, I can get up in the morning. I don't need painkillers. I haven't taken painkillers for months. I was ready to die. I was waiting to die. Now I'm pain free, and nothing is going to stop me! I'm ready to take on the world!

Dave's terminal lung cancer caused total disability

Dave N., a father of four teenage children, got the diagnosis on January 24, 2006. His entire left lung was full of fluid. When the doctor mentioned the "Big C" — cancer — Dave says, "It devastated me – and dropped my wife to the floor."

Because of his lung cancer, Dave couldn't do the things he used to do. He went on full disability. Everything in his life fell apart. By the time the cancer reached Stage Four, he knew he was going to die. The chemo made his face puffy, his eyelids droopy, and also gave him a rash.

Why did Dave make the trip to Reno for cancer treatment? As he explains, "I didn't have a lot of options, and Reno sounded like a good choice." His teenage kids told him, "Dad, we want you to be here. If this is a chance, take it!"

And so Dave decided to undergo the three-week intravenous treatment known as Forsythe Immune Therapy. He says it doesn't hurt, and it doesn't cause hair to fall out.

After three weeks of IV treatment, he went home for three months. Then he returned to Reno for the follow-up exam. As with most of Dr. Forsythe's cancer patients, Dave's treatment lasted four months. Forsythe Immune Therapy is a four-month package.

Stage Four patient says he's "ready to beat the band"!

Dave says, "It felt so warm when I came into Dr. Forsythe's Clinic. Everyone was so friendly." After just the second *day* of intravenous treatment, Dave says, "I was ready to beat the band! I haven't had this kind of energy in almost a year!" And on the third day he felt even better.

According to Dave, "I came up here with a big bag of medications from my doctor back home, and I'm thinking, 'Why am I taking all these things?' I come in here. I'm feeling *great*. There are really no side effects. None. I feel refreshed. I'm ready to go out and, you know, just do anything I can do!"

Dave's wife adds, "Conventional treatment was like a death sentence. There was no hope. Dave lost a lot of hope. Now his mind is different. He's positive. He wants to live."

After the first three weeks of treatment, Dave told us, "I've been doing 20 minute walks. I don't feel like a disabled person anymore. I feel okay. I can walk up and down the street just like anyone else and not be short of breath and have to stop. I feel great."

At Dr. Forsythe's recommendation, Dave dropped sugar from his diet and drinks alkaline water.

When Dave first came to see Dr. Forsythe, the devastating effects of chemotherapy were obvious. Dave's transformation as a result of Forsythe Immune Therapy is remarkable.

Prostate cancer patient gets his sex drive back!

Sadly, some of the conventional treatments for prostate cancer leave a man unable to hold his urine or to get an erection – or both.

But even before Gary M. was treated for advanced prostate cancer, the disease had depressed his sex drive. Instead of submitting to the risks of surgery, he decided to go to Dr. Forsythe's clinic. After ten days of Forsythe Immune Therapy, he could feel the difference.

When Gary returned home, his doctors at the VA hospital examined him. They found no more nodules, no more swelling, no more prostate cancer. In fact, there was no evidence of cancer anywhere anymore.

As for his depressed sex drive, 59-year-old Gary says, "That's no longer a problem."

Testimonials for a wide variety of cancers

During my two-hour interview with Dr. Forsythe, he told me many stories about remarkable recoveries from the most difficult and stubborn cases of cancer. Here are a few of them:

- 52-year-old Paula L. first saw Dr. Forsythe in 2003 for treatment of cancer in her right breast. It had spread to her lungs and bones. As a result of Poly-MVA and other treatments, her tumor markers are normal, and her bone pain is gone. Furthermore, her lung lesions have disappeared. She's in *complete* remission, meaning all measurable signs of disease have disappeared.
- 48-year-old Joseph R. runs a sewage treatment plant in Reno, NV. The cancer in his right lung had spread to his central chest at the time he sought help from Dr. Forsythe. Dr. Forsythe treated him with Poly-MVA and low-dose chemo. Today, the results of his medical tests are normal and he works a 40-hour week without any problems.
- 83-year-old Bob S. was on his deathbed with prostate cancer. After undergoing therapies such as Poly-MVA and low-dose chemo, he's functioning normally. He has no bone pain, he's no longer taking pain medication, and he's walking on his own.
- 81-year-old Warren J. suffered from colorectal cancer that had invaded his lungs and stomach. As a result of treatment with Poly-MVA, he's now free of cancer. His tumor markers are normal.
- 28-year-old Crystal K. suffered from colitis, which turned into colon cancer. Dr. Forsythe treated her with Paw Paw (a nutritional product), Poly-MVA, and vitamins. She's now free of disease and living a normal life.
- 25-year-old Jenna S. had Stage Four Hodgkin's involving her neck and the lymph nodes in her groin. She refused chemotherapy and radiation, and instead sought help from Dr. Forsythe in 2004. He gave her Poly-MVA and persuaded her to take low-dose oral chemotherapy for a short time. She's now off all chemo and in complete remission.
- 44-year-old Sheryl S. from Reno, NV, "flipped" houses when that city enjoyed a hot real estate market. In 2003 she came to see Dr. Forsythe for treatment of Stage Four non-Hodgkin's Lymphoma (NHL). Dr. Forsythe gave her Poly-MVA and other therapies. She is free of disease, and her tumor markers are normal.
- 28-year-old Diedra C., a flight attendant, suffered from ovarian cancer that had spread to her pelvis. In 2004 she came to see Dr. Forsythe, who recommended natural treatments plus low-dose chemo. She's in complete remission and continues to work as a flight attendant. She pays a follow-up visit to Dr. Forsythe twice a year.
- 57-year-old Georgia B. was on her deathbed in 2005. Her cancer doctors recommended that she go into hospice; in other words, they expected her to die soon. But instead of going into hospice, she saw Dr. Forsythe. She didn't want any more chemotherapy because it had failed her. Dr. Forsythe recommended Poly-MVA and other treatments. Now she's in complete remission, running her mattress business with her husband.

Dr. Forsythe has a big advantage over many other doctors. He's fully trained in oncology, but he also has a pathology background. That gives him an intimate knowledge of tumors. A doctor coming from an emergency room background or family practice background would lack this kind of knowledge.

And, as mentioned earlier, he's also a board-certified homeopathic doctor. Dr. Forsythe is one of a kind.

Dr. Forsythe practically swears by the BioMat

To help his patients get rid of toxins, he asks them to lie down on a device called the BioMat. No ordinary mat, its plastic tubules are filled with tourmaline, a semi-precious gem, and expensive amethyst crystals that emit far infrared rays when the mat is powered up.

Dr. Forsythe is convinced that the Japanese-designed BioMat is extremely helpful for detoxifying the body.

He told me, "Using the BioMat is addictive [in a good way]. My wife and I have a far infrared sauna in our house, but we don't use it anymore. Each of us has our own BioMat, which we use instead. We turn the BioMat on a low setting when we go to bed at night, and it stays on all night long.

"Far infrared rays are jumping from the crystals right up through our bodies while we sleep, promoting healing and stimulating the immune system. We flip our BioMats off in the morning. It's great."

The BioMat is manufactured by a company called Richway and costs about $1,500. Dr. Forsythe encourages his patients to buy the BioMat for home use.

An urgent warning about PET/CT scans!

Dr. Forsythe asked me to *emphasize* in this special report that the routine PET/CT scans that most cancer centers use are dangerous. I mentioned this in the first chapter, but it bears repeating: These scans give patients 500 to 600 times the radiation dose of a simple chest X-ray. The excessive radiation beats down a patient's immune cells, which are radio sensitive.

In Dr. Forsythe's opinion, "Giving patients a PET/CT scan every three months to see how the therapy is doing, as major cancer centers do, is self defeating. They don't get it."

Dr. Forsythe's patients come from all over the world

Patients come to Dr. Forsythe's clinic from all over the world – even from as far away as Perth, Australia. "Last week we had two ladies from Nigeria with Stage Four cancer, a patient from Spain with Stage Four prostate cancer, a lady from St. Thomas in the Virgin Islands, and a patient from Canada who has newly diagnosed Stage Four renal cancer," he told me proudly. Not too many doctors in little Reno, Nevada, have that kind of clientele.

Dr. Forsythe said, "In this town of Reno our patients and their companions fill up hotel rooms to the tune of 6,000 per year because they stay three to four weeks. Figure about $100 per day per person: they're spending over $1.7 million a year to the local Reno economy from my clinic alone!"

Dr. Forsythe certainly deserves the Lifetime Achievement Award he received from the Academy of Comprehensive Integrative Medicine on October 13, 2012. These are the concluding words of the award: "Dr. Forsythe, you have blazed a trail for others to follow in integrative oncology. Your ability to stand when attacked has given other practitioners hope. Where lesser men would have retreated, you have forged ahead for the sake of your patients. You have given hope to many who would have otherwise been told to go home and die. For your outstanding leadership and compassion we salute you and acknowledge your life-changing contributions to your fellow man through this award."

Cost of treatment

Each case of cancer differs, so costs will vary, depending on the course of treatment Dr. Forsythe recommends. Insurance may cover some costs, such as the initial consultation and prescription drugs. But insurance does not cover other costs, such as the fee for Dr. Forsythe's Immune Therapy.

When a patient finishes Dr. Forsythe's three week program, he or she is welcome to return to the clinic for follow-up care. But Dr. Forsythe has links with integrative doctors all over the country, enabling his patients to continue good therapy close to home if they prefer. For example, he knows three integrative doctors in Florida.

Where to stay and what to do

Dr. Forsythe's clinic is an outpatient facility, so you'll need to stay at a nearby hotel. Some of these hotels offer special rates for Dr. Forsythe's patients, including the magnificent Vegas-style Peppermill Resort Casino, the similarly spectacular Atlantis Resort Casino, and the Marriott's Residence Inn, which is three miles from the clinic. The Marriott even provides free shuttle service.

As you recover from cancer, you'll probably want to visit nearby Lake Tahoe — perhaps the most stunning mountain lake in the world. It's a jewel. Other nearby sights include historic Virginia City of silver mining fame, and the old Carson City Mint.

Contact information:

James W. Forsythe, M.D., H.M.D.
Century Wellness Clinic
521 Hammill Lane
Reno, Nevada 89511
Phone: 775-827-0707
Toll free: 877-789-0707
Fax: 775-827-1006
Websites: www.CenturyWellness.com
and www.DrForsythe.com

Chapter Five

The doctor who zaps cancer at the clinic that some call "ozone central"

"Adult onset cancer is 100 percent preventable," declares Dr. Frank Shallenberger, M.D., H.M.D., "and I know that because I developed a system to determine how efficiently your body takes in oxygen. Just because you're taking in the oxygen doesn't mean you're efficiently using it. If you're efficiently using oxygen, you're not going to get cancer, period. Never once have I seen a cancer patient using oxygen efficiently. If the key to preventing cancer is using oxygen efficiently, then a key to treating cancer has to do with oxygen!

"You think you don't have cancer? You *have* it. *I* have it. Find a doctor who knows how to measure your oxygen utilization. Get it optimized, then you don't get sick from anything – ever."

What Dr. Shallenberger means, of course, is that everyone produces *some* cancer cells. But the body's normal use of oxygen and the immune system mop up the cancer cells before they become a problem. Oxygen is the key to maintaining health.

That explains why Dr. Shallenberger is so passionate about ozone (O_3), a close cousin of oxygen (O_2). As you may know, oxygen has *two* atoms. Ozone is almost identical except that it has a *third* oxygen atom, which it wants to get rid of because the three-atom oxygen molecule is unstable.

Here's a simple explanation of how ozone works in cancer treatment. You may remember from high school biology that the mitochondria in your cells are the cell's power plants. The mitochondria use oxygen to produce energy. Over 100 years ago, Dr. Otto Warburg discovered that the primary cause of cancer is decreased mitochondrial function: cancer cells thrive in a low-oxygen environment and can't tolerate oxygen.

Here's what Dr. Shallenberger says about ozone:

- Ozone's third oxygen atom stimulates the mitochondria to use oxygen more efficiently.
- Ozone stimulates detoxification; toxins impair mitochondrial function, detoxifying stimulates it.
- Ozone improves blood circulation and stimulates nitric oxide production.
- Ozone forms beneficial peroxides that can last in the body for weeks. (Peroxides are toxic to cancer cells.)
- Ozone in direct contact with a cancer cell will kill it.

In fact, Dr. Shallenberger says there are three key factors in treating cancer: (1) You have to treat the cause; (2) You have to maximize the patient's vitality and immunity; (3) You have to control cancer cell growth.

Amazingly, ozone accomplishes all three.

Ozone therapy is dirt cheap and non-toxic. There are no negative side effects. It's so beneficial and so effective that Dr. Shallenberger can't imagine treating cancer without it. It boggles his mind that cancer patients undergo dangerous and ineffective treatments first instead of starting with the safe and effective methods.

Like the other holistic doctors I interviewed in Nevada, Dr. Shallenberger is double-boarded. That is, he's licensed as an M.D. and also as an H.M.D. (homeopathic medical doctor). The homeopathic license gives him the freedom to treat his patients with natural therapies including nutrition and even laetrile.

Most medical boards and many governmental authorities in America forbid the use of laetrile. Nevada, however, is an oasis of medical freedom because the state recognizes the homeopathic board.

I asked Dr. Shallenberger, "How did you get into holistic medicine?" The story he told is fascinating.

He explained that he started out in medicine almost 40 years ago as an emergency room physician. "I liked it," he said. "The cool thing about it is that you actually fix things as opposed to internal medicine. Those doctors never fix anything. If emergency room doctors practiced medicine the way the other doctors practice, they would treat someone with a knife in his back by giving him some narcotics and sending him home with the knife still in his back!

"In the ER, I was used to people coming in with really bad problems. We fixed the cause, and they left cured – end of story!

The shocking truth about being a family doctor today

"After seven years in the ER, I decided to hang out my shingle and become a family doc. After six months I realized it was bogus because nobody was getting well. I wondered, what's the problem? I was used to people either getting well or dying. But as a family doc, I was dishing out these meds, and patients would come back with the problem not cured and also with side effects from the medicine.

"Seeking advice, I sat down with the chief of the local hospital and asked him, 'What's up with this stuff? I'm getting lousy results. Nobody's getting better. My patients have side effects from the drugs.' He replied, 'Frank you're doing just fine. That's what we all do.' I was incredulous.

"So I created an anonymous questionnaire and circulated it to all the doctors on the medical staff of the hospital in Concord. The questionnaire asked: 'Do you find that you cure most of your patients? What percentage of your patients do you cure? What percentage of your patients get side effects from the drugs you're giving them?' The questionnaires I got back basically said that the doctors didn't cure anybody and that they saw lots of side effects from the drugs. I thought, 'Something's definitely wrong here.'

Revolutionary discovery: medical wisdom from the 1920s

"One day my father, a physician, told me, 'I've got all these old books. You want 'em?' These were medical books from the 1920s and 30s. The modern prescription drug industry didn't really hit until the late 1940s and 50s. Before then, drug companies made vitamins and other natural products. I accepted my father's books. One book was a primer on how to recognize vitamin deficiencies. For example, the book said that sleeplessness, anxiety, and fatigue could point to a deficiency of vitamin B1. That describes just about everyone!

"I kept on prescribing drugs back then, but I also prescribed my patients a hefty B complex pill. And a lot of my patients actually got better! So I became known as the 'vitamin doctor.'

"Fortunately, I learned about a study group Linus Pauling was conducting in San Francisco, just 40 minutes from where I was. I plugged into it. I never even knew about the field of natural medicine. Pauling said disease comes from an imbalance inside your body. You need to treat the imbalance.

"In addition to prescribing my patients B vitamins, I also took them off sugar, and they got better. I came from conventional medicine, but natural medicine flat-out works! With natural medicine, I don't really give a damn *how* it works. I want to know one thing: does it work? The stuff I'm giving out now is pretty harmless. It's not going to hurt anyone. I don't need to know how it works. If the patient gets well, it doesn't matter how it worked.

"I don't just see cancer patients. I see everybody. I don't specialize. That's the way I roll. I treat whoever walks in through the door. I treat cancer, autoimmune diseases, emotional and mental depression, obsessive/compulsive disorders, bipolar disorder. I do a lot of pain management.

"Doc, what's wrong with me?"

"I also help a lot of patients who are all messed up but undiagnosed. They've been to a dozen or more doctors, but none of them can figure out what's wrong. I can almost always get to the bottom of it. I have a cool system I've been teaching for 15 years. If you stay with the system you'll definitely uncover imbalances. There's a certain amount of trial and error. You use lab tests and a physical exam, and you go to the game plan and you fix it. It's not hard. You look for five or six or seven imbalances. It's rare, but maybe once a year someone comes in that I can't fix.

"Chemo isn't good the way conventional oncologists use it. Using chemo all by itself is too harsh. I treat cancer with *low dose* chemo and other therapies. I like it. I think it works just great. I sometimes throw radiation in too. I also see a lot of people who are getting conventional chemo, and they see me, too. So I'm incorporating the holistic stuff the conventional oncologist isn't doing. I help minimize side effects.

"The way I see it, chemo kills cancer cells 80 percent of the time, but they come back. And the patient suffers. These are the issues we focus on: Why is the cancer coming back, what can we do to stop it from coming back, and how can we minimize the patient's suffering? Herbs can help a lot with suffering.

Too much chemo turns patients into zombies

"We use Insulin Potentiating Therapy (IPT) with low dose chemo, and we don't see harsh side effects. My chemo nurse for a while had a 2nd job in the oncology unit at the local hospital, which has an IV room like ours. She told me, 'You ought to see it. Here people are bright and bubbly, but in the IV room over at the hospital, they look like a bunch of zombies. They're all messed up.'"

IPT makes use of insulin as a sort of Trojan horse, to "fool" cancer cells into taking in vastly greater amounts of a toxic chemotherapy drug than do healthy cells. The therapy is based on the fact that cancer cells have an extraordinary appetite for glucose (blood sugar) and possess ten times the number of insulin receptors that healthy cells do. This enables cancer cells to metabolize sugar at a much higher rate.

When insulin is administered to a cancer patient at the same time as a chemo drug, the multiple insulin receptors on cancer cells open wide and take up the chemotherapy drug at very high rate compared to healthy cells. Thanks to this, the doctor can achieve a lethal effect on cancer cells many times greater than that felt by healthy cells.

Because insulin multiplies the power of a chemo drug, the doctor can use a lower dose of the drug and avoid damaging healthy cells the way full-dose chemotherapy does. Yet IPT damages cancer cells just as much as a high dose of chemo delivered with the insulin boost.

Dr. Shallenberger had this to say about the damage chemo can do: "I'll see some side effects from using one tenth of the conventional dose of chemo, and I think, 'What would happen if the patient got 10 times this dose?' It would be freaky. I'd be scared to do it. We lessen the patient's suffering by giving the lower dose. And even though it's one tenth the dose, I believe it works every bit as well as the higher dose in killing cancer cells.

Sometimes it's enough just to control cancer

"What can we do to keep cancer from coming back? How can we control it? In some cases, we can't completely get rid of the cancer, but we can achieve stable disease [in which the immune system keeps the cancer in check]. We have a lot of patients out there playing golf in a state of stable disease, and you'd never know there was anything wrong with them because they have their health. Now, if you look at their CT scan you'd see cancer all over the place, but the cancer isn't doing anything, and they have a decent quality of life. They just have to watch themselves and come into my office once in a while to keep their cancer under control.

"Some patients come in with Stage Four cancer and have the expectation: 'I want the cancer gone so I can get back to my life exactly the way it was before.' Like: 'Take the wart off.'

"I have an honest discussion with these patients, telling them, 'There's a one-in-three or one-in-four chance you'll be cured in the sense that you want to be cured. You have Stage Four disease. If you were seeing a conventional oncologist anywhere in the world, your chances would be one-in-40 that you'd be alive in five years. You can't go back to your life as it was before.

"'You have a two-volume life. Volume I is your life before you got cancer. And Volume II is after you were diagnosed with cancer, and it's going to be a different story. You have to grasp that and get hold of it. And when you do, we can get to work.'

"Here in America we have two kinds of treatment. One is safe, inexpensive, and harmless, and the other is expensive and dangerous. Most people resort to the expensive and dangerous treatment first, and if that doesn't work, then they go to the safe and harmless treatment. It should be the other way around. It's silly that insurance companies pay for the expensive and dangerous treatments but not for the safe and inexpensive treatments.

"Most oncologists don't care what their patients eat, whether it's ice cream all day or Twinkies for every meal [even though sugar feeds cancer] – as long as the patients are getting calories.

Ingenious ways Dr. Shallenberger uses ozone

"I'm big into ozone here. I've written a book about it: *Principles and Applications of Ozone Therapy: A Practical Guideline for Physicians*. We do ozone every which way. Ozone has marvelous detox effects. It will cause the body to release toxins dramatically. It kills infections, which are almost always a part of all diseases including cancer. It beefs up the immune system and strengthens anti-oxidant defenses. This is all proven, not conjecture. It's the perfect therapy to give for just about any disease there is.

"This medical office is ozone central. We take blood out, treat the blood with ozone, and return the blood to the patient. We inject ozone gas directly into the vein. We inject ozone gas into the intestines, into the vagina, into the tissues, right into tumors, and around tumors. We inject ozone into the CSF spinal fluid. We can put it into bladders for bladder cancer. We can basically put ozone any damn place we want to put it. We can run a nasogastric tube into a patient's stomach and shoot ozone to kill stomach cancer. And we do all of it!

"I have a colonic hydrotherapist on staff. Colonic hydrotherapy helps the liver detox. I love colonics. When people are on chemo, they're getting a colonic pretty much every day. And when she gives a colonic, she's pumping in ozone, so they're getting an ozone treatment in the rectum. After that they go down the hallway into the ozone sauna [a steam sauna with the body enclosed in the sauna unit except for the patient's head] and they absorb ozone through the skin for 45 minutes. And then they go down the hallway and get ozone through the blood.

"Ozone reacts to double bonds. When I inject ozone into the rectum, within seconds, it's gone. It no longer exists. It has reacted with the double bonds of the mucosa of the rectum in the intestines and formed peroxides. The peroxides last for days or weeks. In the sauna, except for your head, your skin gets coated with ozone gas, and your skin is alive with peroxides. When you get out of the ozone sauna, you smell like ozone gas, and your entire skin surface is 100 percent peroxide.

"If you bubble ozone through olive oil, you can then inhale the vapors from that – the peroxides. You can't inhale ozone directly but you can inhale the peroxides. A guy with lung cancer is now doing that. You can also put ozone into the ears so that it reacts with the tympanic membrane to form the peroxides that promote healing even in the ear canals and sinuses. Our use of ozone is maybe the most unique thing about this clinic.

"I use the Riordan formula for vitamin C. I like Poly-MVA [a highly regarded, proprietary food supplement]. I use laetrile orally and intravenously for leukemia or lymphoma that doesn't respond to IPT. Leukemia responds well to ozone.

At last, a non-addictive solution to chronic pain

"Ozone is also very good for pain! I developed a technique 20 years ago where I pre-inject an area with Novocain and some nutrients including sugar and some B vitamins, and then I inject ozone. I can inject it into the knees, hips, shoulders, practically any area that hurts. And it'll pretty much get rid of the pain."

Dr. Shallenberger has had a lot of success with prostate cancer and breast cancer because those comprise most of the cases he sees. He also does well with other cancers, including colon cancer.

A man from Alaska came to Dr. Shallenberger's clinic with a tube in his stomach. He had esophageal cancer and couldn't swallow his saliva. He'd dropped 30 or 40 pounds. He was in terrible shape except for one good thing: he hadn't undergone any conventional treatment, which would've compromised his immune system.

The conventional oncologist in Alaska told him, "You're too far gone to treat. We can't help you." He replied to the oncologist, "I'm going to come back here and give you this feeding tube."

Terminal patient shocks his oncologist

The patient kept his word. After Dr. Shallenberger helped him beat his cancer, the patient pulled out his feeding tube and went back to Alaska to give it to the oncologist.

Another man, named Kenny, came in to see Dr. Shallenberger three years ago. He had squamous cell carcinoma of the throat – a tough, deadly cancer. Dr. Shallenberger helped him shrink the cancer down to a manageable size. He still has cancer, but he's in a state of stable disease. "If you saw Kenny, you'd have no idea anything was wrong with him," said Dr. Shallenberger. "He pops in here every six weeks."

A walking health disaster survived his cancer and thrives!

A man named Jack had colon cancer that had spread far and wide. "Jack astounds me even today," Dr. Shallenberger told me. "He had diabetes, was overweight, and he smoked. He was the most unfit human being you've ever seen in your life.

"When he came in here he was on crutches. His foot was in a cast because he had a big diabetic ulcer with osteomyelitis on his foot. He'd also had part of his colon removed after a previous bout with cancer, and now the cancer was back and had spread to his liver. I gave him about two minutes to live.

"As bad as Jack's lifestyle was, he never worried about anything. He and his wife decided to get serious about juicing and detox, and they made it to all of their appointments. His cancer went away. The biofilm infection on his foot cleared up after ozone treatments. Biofilms are filled with double bonds, and ozone just eats them up. I told him to keep coming back, but he never did. But Jack's wife traveled through here a month ago, almost two years after I'd last seen him. I was glad to hear her say he was doing just fine.

"We work with people where they are. I'm just here to help people. I'll still help them even if they want to be helped in their own way."

One of the most affordable clinics in America

Dr. Shallenberger said his whole program – an intensive three weeks of therapy, which includes two IPT treatments per week, PolyMVA, the whole shebang – costs $4,000 per week. That's more than reasonable. And patients get insurance reimbursement for the chemotherapy part of the treatment, and for doctor's visits, though there's no insurance reimbursement for such treatments as ozone, colonics, and IVs other than hydration IVs.

Dr. Shallenberger's clinic is one of the most affordably priced holistic clinics in America. It's a pleasant, cheerful place to get well. The IV room has large windows, allowing the patients to enjoy the mountain vista while they chat with each other.

Patients stay at a hotel down the street for about $175 per week. The hotel rooms have kitchenettes, and organic food and juicing supplies are available in Reno, which is 45 minutes away. The hotel shuttles the patients to the clinic unless patients prefer to drive a rental car.

It's worth mentioning that the U.S. mint in Carson City minted millions of dollars worth of coins during the silver bonanza. The old mint building is now a museum. Because I'm a history buff, I visited it and recommend it to others.

Contact information:

Dr. Frank Shallenberger, M.D., H.M.D.
The Nevada Center of Alternative & Anti-Aging Medicine
1231 Country Club Drive
Carson City, NV 89703
775-884-3990
www.AntiAgingMedicine.com

Chapter Six

The amazing Persian doctor who beats "hopeless" cases of cancer with natural methods

Ferre Akbarpour, M.D., has been turning around "hopeless" and "terminal" cases of cancer in Southern California for decades. Her clinic occupies the entire ninth floor of the Pacifica Tower, the tallest office building in Huntington Beach.

Her patients love the panoramic view of the Pacific Ocean, Catalina Island, and the mountains. But they love Dr. Ferre (pronounced "fairy") and her lifesaving treatments even more.

We visited Dr. Ferre in her office, and she generously let us interview her. She did such a fine job of telling her story that we decided simply to print it as she told it to us:

Dr. Ferre's story in her own words

I have been here in Southern California since 1978. Every day I get three or four thank you letters from patients. It's really amazing. It's so positively energizing. It's just unbelievable.

I thank God for allowing me to be in this field and do what I'm doing now. It's important for me to read these letters. And it gives me so much energy to help even more patients overcome cancer.

Let me tell you a memorable story. About six and a half years ago a gentleman named Robert came to me from Australia with Stage Four colon cancer. Stage Four means that it has spread to some other places. Most doctors consider it terminal. Doctors didn't give him more than two or three months to live. That's why he decided to come here.

Robert was short of money, so his local church donated money to pay for his treatment. Some people at his church had heard about our success rate with advanced cancer patients. So he came here with his beautiful wife and with his good sense of humor.

When I asked him, "Robert, what Stage are you at?" He said, "Stage Five." I said, "There is no such thing as Stage Five. Either it is a Stage One or Two or Three or Four." He said, "No, doctor. The cancer has spread to all my organs, so I think I'm above a Stage Four."

And then he said, "I know I'm going to get better." I didn't give him any promises because it's not ethical. You don't know that will happen with late-stage cancer. I said, "I promise I'll do my best. Let us start working on you."

This man's colon cancer had spread to the kidneys, liver, bladder, and even the lungs. He was in terrible shape. He had elevated liver enzymes. He had lost a lot of weight. And he had severe fatigue and jaundice. Furthermore, he couldn't go for any more oncological treatments because he had maxed out all the chemotherapies.

So we started working on him. Thank God, he improved a lot. After staying with us for four weeks, it became obvious he was getting better and better. So the church donated more money, enabling him to stay longer — about seven or eight weeks. And then he went back to Australia.

From the brink of the grave to the golf course!

For a man who was given two months to live, he lived for four-and-a-half extra years. And the beauty is that he was able to do what he loved: play golf. He was enjoying his life at the ocean in Australia, and he was happily married. He was traveling; he was doing everything he enjoyed. A few days before he passed away, he called me. I was constantly in touch with him. We were emailing. We were having phone consultations.

I was changing his protocols. I was ordering blood work.

So a few days before he passed away, he called me and said, "Doctor Ferre, it looks like I'm ready to go." He was dying not of cancer but of kidney failure, and dialysis wasn't going well. So he said, "I think I want to say goodbye to you. I'm really thankful that you gave me the opportunity to live four-and-a-half years. I have been the happiest person."

The day he passed away, his wife sent us an email. She said, "Robert passed away, but I wanted to thank you for the years you gave us. Robert lived happier, healthier, and he was stronger spiritually, physically, and emotionally since he was under your care. And I wanted to thank you for that."

So this is a memorable story. It will always be in my mind and in my heart.

Farmer beats deadliest lung cancer

I had a farmer from Connecticut come to us with one of the deadliest cancers of the lung. He kept saying, "If I die, I've lived a good life. If I live, I'll be thankful to God." He wasn't afraid of dying.

This beautiful man came with his daughter. He was here at least four weeks. He started to do better and better and better. Conventional medicine offers no treatments for this kind of cancer — no chemo, no radiation, nothing — because the cancer is not sensitive to anything. So the only thing that helped him was our natural treatment.

We were so proud of him; we had his CAT scans, taking them everywhere and showing them to others. And with this treatment, he got better and better and better. The tumor totally disappeared, as proven by a CAT scan. He did so well that he went back home and went back to work. Three years passed. It's unheard of for anyone to survive this kind of lung cancer for three years! Three years passed, so we were all so happy and so proud.

His lung cancer never did come back. He later died of another cause.

Young dentist thought his life was ruined by nasopharyngeal cancer

I have a written testimonial of a young dentist. He came to me in August of 2005 with an unfortunate case of nasopharyngeal cancer. That's one of the worst cancers, not only because of its gravity but also because of the way it progresses. Conventional doctors can't do much for these patients. Also, because it occupies the oral cavity — ear, nose, and throat — usually the patients become deformed and lose their hearing, their speech, and their ability to eat.

So it's one of the worst cancers that people could ever get.

This dentist was practicing in Texas. He was going to one of the most prestigious cancer clinics in Texas, and the treatment seemed to be successful.

But one day when he was playing ball with his six-year-old son, his son accidentally kicked him in the groin. So he started to have pain and swelling. He went to his doctor and said, "Listen, this is hurting too much." A CAT scan revealed that his cancer was back and had spread to his abdomen. It was bad.

Dentist says NO to chemo and prepares for death

The doctor told him, "Let's start chemotherapy immediately. We may squeeze two or three months out of your life." He said, "No, thank you, I don't want to do it." He had been through chemo before, and he didn't want any more of it — especially since the chemo only offered him another two or three months.

The dentist had already made plans to move to California. Thinking he was healthy, he had sold his dental practice in Texas and had already purchased a major dental clinic in California. All of a sudden, his plans lay in ruins.

He came to California anyway but couldn't practice dentistry because of his ill health. One of his friends, a religious woman, told him, "Go and see this lady. I've heard a lot of good things about her."

So he came to see me in August of 2005. He was sitting there with his wife. I tried speaking to him, but he seemed out of it — as if he were thinking, "I'm dying. What's this lady talking about?" So I talked to his wife. His wife said, "We're starting with you tomorrow."

The man started with me. He was here for three weeks. Every day he felt better and better and better. Then I told him, "Let's do genetic testing analysis for your cancer. Let us send your blood to Germany for some genetic analysis, and they will do the gene testing and they will let us know what kind of treatment your body would best respond to."

So we did that, we sent it to Germany. The results came back, showing that his cancer was ultra-sensitive to hyperthermia. He was already receiving hyperthermia every day. It also indicated that his cancer was sensitive to a certain kind of chemo. He was against chemo because of his past experience with it. But I assured him he would have no problem with a low dosage. He said OK.

With my treatment and the low-dosage chemo, he responded well. The lymph nodes got smaller, he was in no pain, and he didn't have any recurrence in the nasopharyngeal area. He's in total remission and went back to work. I have a lot of cases like this.

Opera singer miraculously recovers her voice

I had a patient from Texas named Bernadette. She came to me again about seven or eight years ago. She had multiple problems including cancer.

One of Bernadette's major problems was Guillain-Barré Syndrome, which paralyzed her extremities and also the muscles of her lungs. She had been an opera singer but no longer had enough lung power to sing. She had lived in hospitals for the previous 12 years. And they had done everything that standard medicine has available — even a high dosage of a steroid therapy. But they couldn't help her.

Amidst this agony, she came down with serious muscle aches and muscle pain. So she got hooked on morphine and morphine derivatives. And she became addicted to all these narcotics.

I'll never forget. She called me and she said, "Doctor, I'm coming for detoxification because I have Guillain-Barré syndrome and I am hooked on these medications. Can you help me?" I said, "I'll try." She said, "How long do you need me?" I said, "At least two weeks to detox your body and blood."

So she came here. After five working days, she said, "Doctor, I don't think my body even desires any narcotics any more. I think I've forgotten all about narcotics. I'm doing fine without them. And my muscles are getting stronger. I'm able to breathe better. I don't need oxygen, and I am just feeling stronger!"

Her second week of treatment took place during Thanksgiving. I told some patients, "I'd better leave earlier today for my TV interview." And Bernadette just stood up and said, "Can I come with you?" I said, "Yes, of course you can. But it's a Persian program, and you don't speak Persian." She said, "But someone could translate my message. I want to come and tell the world. Since it's Thanksgiving, I want to share my blessing with the world and let them know there's still hope left."

So I took her with me. Another doctor was the host. I was that doctor's guest. And he interviewed Bernadette, who told him about her amazing health results.

When the doctor realized Bernadette was an opera singer who hadn't been able to sing for years, he asked, "Do you think you could sing now?" She replied, "Sing? Oh, my gosh. I don't think so. But I'll try." And she started to sing opera. I was crying. She was crying. She was hugging me. That was such an emotional thing.

Bernadette beats melanoma with *totally natural* remedies

That's not even all. During this time she was diagnosed with malignant melanoma, a serious cancer of the skin. She was concerned she wasn't going to survive the melanoma. She started to eat healthy. She continued with detoxification and other therapies. And then I started her on immune boosting for her melanoma.

Melanoma is a disease that spreads *quickly*. But it didn't spread anywhere in her body, and she recovered from melanoma. Melanoma is a cancer that responds beautifully to immune boosting. And we did that with non-chemical, totally natural remedies, *totally natural.*

And her anemia got better. Her melanoma has never come back, which her oncologist confirmed. She is in total remission with her melanoma. And the good news is that she got married last year in a beautiful castle in Scotland. Her husband is from Scotland.

In fact, she wants me to put her wedding picture on my website. She said, "Doctor, I beg you, please do that." She's that thankful to me. It's so beautiful, so beautiful.

And I talked with her four or five days ago, and she said, "I have never felt this good in my life. I'm going to school, and I'm right now doing everything myself. But I have so much energy, and I'm doing so much better." She's still taking my supplements. She's still under my direction for supplementation and everything.

And another beautiful thing is that since she improved so much with all these natural treatments that I am doing, she is becoming a naturopathic doctor herself. She is going through the second year of naturopathic school, and she said in a few years she's going to become a doctor.

Doctors said her bilateral ovarian cancer was "hopeless"

Three years ago a young lady came to see me from San Francisco. She was about 45 years old and never married. She told me she wasn't from a rich family. She said she really needed my help.

I had helped her niece get rid of a spinal tumor. That's how she knew me.

So her brother-in-law, the father of the girl who got rid of the spinal tumor, told her he was going to sell his laundromat, get some money, and send her to me. Her doctors said her case was "hopeless."

At the time of diagnosis, the cancer had already spread *all over her abdomen.* The tumor was so big they couldn't even do surgery. And she was afraid of chemotherapy. And she told me her doctors had drawn at least 12 or 13 liters of fluid from her lungs and abdomen. Her cancer marker was close to 4,000 when we started with her. A normal marker is not more than 35.

So this was an unfortunate case.

Crying patient says, "I don't want to die"

When she first came here, she cried all the time. She put her head on my shoulder and cried, saying, "I don't want to die. I don't want to die." And I told her, "Listen, no one is God, and I don't want to promise you too much, but we're doing our best. You've got to stay positive. Don't lose your faith. Stay positive. Good things will happen."

So during her first week of treatment I had to give her a lot of encouragement and spiritual support.

The second week she realized the treatment was helping her because she wasn't accumulating water anymore. She wasn't bloated. She was feeling better, less nauseous. She could breathe better. There was no more fluid in her lungs.

Since her case was so bad, I told her, "Listen, I want you to understand that I'm your support. We need a combination treatment here. We need to integrate the standard treatment with what we are doing because of the seriousness of your case."

She started to cry and said, "I'm scared the chemotherapy is going to kill me." I said, "No. I'm going to send you to another oncologist, and I promise we are going to start you with the lowest dosage of chemotherapy. And if you tolerate it and you feel okay with that, then we are going to go to the standard dosage."

And that's what we did with her.

She trusted me and agreed to go see another oncologist. We started the combination chemotherapy and my natural treatments at the same time together. And, thank God, because she was getting our natural treatments, she didn't have too many side effects. She didn't have much fatigue, nausea, or loss of appetite.

So she was with us for four weeks. And then we sent her back to her oncologist and surgeon in San Francisco. The surgeon did a scan. Amazingly, the tumor had shrunk in just four weeks. And the cancer markers had dropped to almost less than half in one month. So the oncological surgeon told her, "Now we can do surgery." She survived and she came back to normal life in no time. No complications, no problems.

Again, two or three months later, after she improved from her surgery, she came back here. I gave her more treatment; I sent her back to her chemotherapy. In less than six or seven months she was in total remission. Her cancer has never returned. She's alive and doing fine. This is another beautiful story.

Doctors called his lung cancer "hopeless"

Seven or eight years ago I helped a man overcome advanced prostate cancer. He did fine.

Then three years ago he called me all of a sudden. His situation was sad. He came in with his wife and told me, "Unfortunately, I was just diagnosed with lung cancer a month ago. In surgery they removed a little bit, but they said I'm in Stage Three to Four. It has gone to the lymph nodes. They don't have too much hope for me. You saved my life once before, and I want you to help me."

Again, I did the same thing with him. He was here for five weeks. He was in bad shape, coughing a lot. He had multiple tumors.

He started to get stronger and better every day. He was coughing less. After three weeks I told him, "Mike, I want you to see another oncologist and let us try a *small* dosage of some chemotherapy, because there are some chemotherapy patients with lung cancer who are doing fine with it, and yours is the kind that may respond."

So he said, "Doctor, if you think so, I will." I told him, "If it doesn't work or you can't tolerate it, we'll just stop." He trusted me.

The tumor shrank so much that he was able to go for another surgery. This time they were able to remove it. Again he came back for my treatment after the tumor was removed, and he got my treatment for another month.

And at Christmastime he came here. He said, "You gave me the gift of life, Doctor Ferre. I can't thank you enough. I'm back to my work. No one believed I was going to survive this cancer." That was three years ago.

Patients need hope, but not false hope

Sometimes I see patients who've maxed out their chemotherapy and radiation therapy. Some of them have also had unsuccessful multiple surgeries. And then they come to me. These are bad cases.

And when I see the patients with nearly hopeless cases, I try to give them hope. I don't tell them "I'm going to cure you." I will tell them "I'm going to do my best." I have had some patients who did well. I have had some patients who didn't do too well because they came too late. So I'm honest with my patients.

You know, there have been lots of times when I sit and cry with my patients. These people are hopeless. Sometimes they don't even have any family support left. So they come here on their own. They have no one else. And I help them and talk with them.

Patients pray and meditate in clinic's chapel

We pray together. We have a little chapel in our clinic. Our patients go there no matter what religion they have. Just the connection with your Creator is important. Some people go there to pray. Some meditate. Some have their private time with their family. They do whatever gives them comfort.

We ask them to have prayer in their daily program because I strongly believe if you want to treat a patient successfully, you have to believe in the connection of mind, body, and spirit. If you don't have these connected together, then you cannot treat any diseases.

I'm a strong believer in Hippocrates, the Father of Medicine. Amazingly, medical science is now proving Hippocrates right. For example, Hippocrates said the best way to treat disease is through the immune system. And he talked about the need for harmony and unity. He said if you want to be healthy, your mind and body must be in harmony with your environment.

Can you believe he said those things 2,500 years ago?

You can give a patient the best treatment, but if he has disharmony with his God or his family or his past, or if he has too much stress at work, the patient won't do well.

I tell my patients, "This is the time for you to be at peace. You have to allocate all your energies to getting better. This is the healing time. You have to forget about anything that bothered you. And you have to have forgiveness. That way, your body and your spirit and your mind are going to be in harmony."

If these things are in harmony, no matter what kind of disease the patients have, they're going to have better success in fighting that disease.

So I bring this to my patients' attention. If they need any spiritual healing, they let me know. I will find help for them. I have psychologists and spiritual healers who work with my cancer patients. They work on the mind, body, and spirit. And they get so much better. They feel so much better.

And of course I'm the one who focuses on the patient's body. I check their immune system and their kidney/liver function. I check them for anemia and for antioxidant deficiency. I check their Vitamin D level and their electrolytes. I'm monitoring them constantly.

And I have two doctors who are working with me for my research. So if I need the latest article, for example, about brain tumors or skin tumors or anything like that, they deliver it to me immediately.

I try to use the best of everything from all over the world. There may be something a doctor in Israel is doing that I didn't know about. And then I ask my research doctors to find it for me. They bring it to me, and the new research may influence me to adjust the treatment. I try to be on top of all the newest information so I can do the best.

Natural treatment secrets revealed

The treatments I give are *totally natural.*

Number one, when the patients start with me, I check all their body functions. I check their kidney, liver, heart — everything.

And then I start with the daily treatments. I start with massage therapy for 45 to 60 minutes for lymphatic drainage. I have a certified massage therapist who gives this therapy, which helps relax the patients throughout the day. So they start with massage therapy, and they love it. And they look forward to that massage therapy every single day.

Why do I feel so strongly that massage therapy is necessary? It's because all these patients with cancer or chronic diseases are toxic. If their bodies were not toxic they wouldn't have gotten the disease. And most have gone through chemotherapy, which results in a lot of toxins in their body. So the massage and the consequent lymphatic drainage are not only going to relax them, but also help them get rid of toxins.

And the lady who gives the massage is also going to give them some reflexology. And that is something else that the patients look forward to because it balances their energy and helps them get rid of pain. They love it.

So this is a key part of the treatment: Massage therapy, lymphatic drainage, detoxification, and reflexology.

Right after massage therapy, the patients go into the infrared sauna. It's a special kind of sauna that helps the patients detoxify. And the beauty of it is that even the patients with lung disease and heart disease can tolerate the heat of the infrared sauna. Of course, a nurse or one of the doctors watches the patients during their time in the infrared sauna. They start with 10 or 15 minutes a day in the sauna, and then as they tolerate it we increase the timing.

And usually we give them about 20 minutes in the infrared sauna.

Cancer hates heat!

Why do I do this? It relaxes the patients as they get rid of the toxins through sweating and perspiration. But the most important reason is that *cancer cells hate the heat.* So the infrared sauna helps weaken the cancer cells, making them easier to kill off.

After the infrared sauna, the patients get intravenous therapy for three or four hours. I give them multiple minerals and some antioxidants intravenously — especially a high dosage of Vitamin C. That's because Vitamin C in high doses has a toxic effect on cancer cells without hurting the healthy cells. The Vitamin C helps release hydrogen peroxide into the cancer cells, and the hydrogen peroxide is going to act like a cancer-killing substance.

This IV therapy is a safe way of doing something for these patients. It strengthens the immune system while weakening the cancer cells. So if the patient also gets chemotherapy the result will be better than with chemotherapy alone.

While patients are getting this IV therapy, they are going to be relaxing in a spacious room. I don't have a crowd of patients. I don't take more than five patients per week. The patients are friendly with each other. They have TV sets, and I encourage them to watch comedies because laughter boosts the immune system. We have a good selection of comedies, or they can watch a movie they bring from home.

The patients can also enjoy a spectacular panoramic view of the Pacific Ocean, Catalina Island, and the mountains from our floor-to-ceiling windows on the ninth floor.

Helping patients visualize whipping cancer

Also I show them a video cartoon that helps patients visualize their own healthy immune cells destroying their cancer cells. Watching this video really energizes and encourages them. It really gives them a positive attitude that they're going to whip their cancer.

Let's face it. When someone is diagnosed with cancer, the big "C," it's scary. A lot of times patients lose it. They lose their positive attitude. They think cancer is going to take their lives. But when I show them the animated cartoon of the immune system killing cancer cells, they realize a strong immune system can destroy their cancer cells." [Editor's note: See Chapter 11 about Dr. O. Carl Simonton for more information about this powerful visualization technique for healing.]

After the first IV is finished, we give them the second IV — a natural supplement we get from Canada. This supplement is an extract of ginseng. It's expensive. To make just one bottle of it takes at least 100 pounds of ginseng! It's that potent.

And then there's a third IV that prolongs the effect of the Vitamin C.

So these are things that patients will do every day.

In addition, we do a nutritional consultation. Our certified nutritionist is one of the best. She has helped a lot of emaciated patients — patients who've lost a lot of weight because of cancer or AIDS. She sees the patients and their families, spending at least an hour with them to explain the importance of diet.

Cancer's best friend: sugar!

For example, I truly take the sugar out of my cancer patients' diet. And before they see me, most patients have no idea why sugar is so bad. And not only do I explain it to them, but other doctors who work with me also talk with them about the importance of diet.

My nutritionist explains that the cancer cells have more receptors for sugar than a normal cell. So eating less sugar weakens the patient's cancer cells. Cutting out sugar is sometimes tough for patients because sugar and sweets are delicious. Our dietician gives them recipes. Patients can see the dietician as many times as they want.

And then we start the patients on a lot of natural supplements. Some supplements are for detoxification. Some supplements help build the patients' strength. This is especially important for patients who have pancreatic cancers, since they're nauseous and vomiting a lot. These patients are weak. I give some patients food supplements high in calories and protein. My cancer patients take a lot of supplements.

Diabetic patients get different supplements for their diabetes, and I have a lot of supplements for immune boosting. That's important.

And some of the supplements are going to be used to repair damaged DNA. It took a scientist 25 years to develop one such supplement, which is proven to work through studies in mice and even in human beings. If DNA is damaged, it can initiate cancer. So we want to prevent further damage.

And also I have an all-natural supplement that blocks circulation to the cancer cells. This supplement has a lot of science behind it. It has been studied and compared with standard medications. It's totally safe and far less expensive than the standard drugs. And it has no side effects.

I tell the patients, "We want to help your body. Let's see what your own body is going to do with your cancer."

In addition to the massage therapy, infrared sauna, IVs, and oral supplementation, we use hyperthermia. Patients enjoy going into the hyperthermia tent, which raises the body temperature. This helps them detoxify, and cancer hates heat. All of our equipment is approved by the FDA or registered by the FDA.

[Editor's note: In one of our other Special Reports, *Natural Cancer Remedies that Work*, Dr. Morton Walker devotes an entire chapter to the story of hyperthermia, including how it was discovered, what the treatment is like, and how it literally cooks cancer out of the body. Visit: www.naturalcancerremedies.com.]

Natural treatments are included in one flat fee

The natural treatments we give here at our clinic cost a flat fee of $5,900 per week. We inform the patients that insurance doesn't pay for our treatments. Rather, they'll be paying out of pocket. Of course, they could pay by credit card or check. And that includes all the natural treatments from the time they start until they leave.

No one is going to be left unattended. Sometimes I give them about $2,000 per week in oral supplements. I use expensive stuff — the finest that money can buy. I don't care about the money. I seek the best quality. So I'm not going to sacrifice quality to try to get the price down. I'm just going to give my patients the best, period. So it's all included: the dietician, the massage therapist, the infrared sauna, the IVs, the hyperthermia, and everything else is included in that $5,900.

The only thing we don't pay for is the lab work, which is covered by the patient's insurance. Since I'm a licensed medical doctor, we have never had any problem with the lab work for our patients. And insurance normally covers that.

If patients are at Stage One or Two, they may be here for only a couple of weeks. In that case we give them detoxification and advice for diet, supplementation, and IV treatments.

But if they come to me at Stage Three or Four, they're really in bad shape. In that case I'll probably need to treat them for four weeks. A few of these patients are in good shape after just three weeks. If I'm satisfied they're getting stronger, their liver function is getting better, and they're able to continue their supplement treatment at home, I will tell them three weeks is enough. But with the Stage Fours, usually I will keep them for four weeks.

I believe that combining the best of both alternative medicine and standard medicine makes good integrative medicine. That's how we're going to save the patient's life.

Contact information:

Dr. Ferre Akbarpour, M.D.
The Orange County Immune Institute
Pacifica Tower
18800 Delaware Street, Suite 900
Huntington Beach, CA 92648
Phone: 714-842-1777
Email: drferre@drferre.com
Website: www.drferre.com

Unforgettable love story

How a Persian doctor in California saved a dying six-year-old Iranian girl and found love at first sight

Editor's note: Ferre Akbarpour, M.D., got her education in Persia but has practiced medicine in Southern California since 1978. Iraj Kiani, an oil tycoon who was based in London, told us the remarkable story of how a desperate Iranian mother found healing for her dying six-year-old daughter. We transcribed his riveting remarks, which appear below:

By Iraj Kiani

It happened November 1, 2001. On that day my life was turned upside down.

I had just flown in from Zurich to London to prepare for a multimillion dollar oil deal. I was supposed to leave the next day for West Africa. The president of one of the African countries wanted to discuss a big oil deal with me, since I had the right to explore and produce gas and oil in that country.

I came home that night. I was alone, relaxing with a drink and getting myself ready to go out for dinner and thereafter to fly to Africa. I turned on the TV to watch the Iranian channel. I saw a doctor on the TV, talking about a drug that had just been approved by the FDA for actually curing leukemia. After discussing the drug, he opened the telephone lines to the public if they had any questions.

The first caller was a lady calling all the way from Iran. She was crying so hard she had trouble speaking properly.

She asked that doctor, "How can I get this drug? My six-year-old daughter was diagnosed with leukemia last year. We've spent all of our money for the treatment of my daughter, but it didn't work. And my daughter now is dying in front of my eyes. Please tell me where I can get this drug and how much is it?"

Mother loses all hope for her six-year-old girl's recovery

The doctor replied, "The drug is available in America, but unfortunately it is a little bit expensive: about $3,300 a month." And the poor woman was still crying when she said, "Doctor, I'm from a poor family, and I can't afford even to buy this drug for one month." And the doctor said, "I'm sorry. I'm just a scientist. I can't do anything for you."

The poor woman continued to cry and, without even saying goodbye, she hung up on him.

I knew the owner of that TV station. So I picked up the phone and asked to speak to the owner. I told him, "I have an offer for you, but I want you to promise me that you won't mention my name on the TV." He gave me his word. So I said, "Here's the deal. I'm going to give you my credit card number. As long as I'm alive I want to buy that drug every month and send it to this poor woman to save her baby's life."

He started asking me and begging me to let him mention my name on the air. I said, "No. I'm not doing it for publicity. I'm doing it for my heart. I'm doing it for my God."

URGENT message for the desperate, crying mother!

The TV station owner went on the air in front of the camera and said, "Ladies and gentlemen, I'm sorry to interrupt the program, but I have an URGENT message for the lady who was crying a few minutes ago because she was not able to buy a cancer drug for her baby. Please call us immediately. Call us back. I know a gentleman who wants to be a sponsor of your baby and buy the drug for your baby. Call us."

Because a child's life was at stake, I called the chief protocol for the African head of state to postpone my meeting. I said, "Please tell the President I cannot be there tomorrow." And that president is famous; when he gets angry he's like a tiger. I don't want to mention his name or his country. It wasn't easy to postpone that appointment because I knew the delay would irritate him.

I couldn't think about the money, the oil deal, or meeting the President. I just wanted to accomplish my mission to save the girl's life. I had to follow my heart, no matter what.

I was supposed to go out for dinner that night, but I cancelled that, too.

My phone rang. The call was long distance from Iran. It was the poor woman who had cried over her dying daughter. We spoke for an hour and a half.

"Are you human or an angel?"

The mother's first question to me was, "Who are you?" I said, "Ma'am, my name is Iraj Kiani." She said, "No, I mean, are you a human? Are you an angel? Why do you want to help my daughter?" I said, "Just consider that this is a mission from God. Give me your number and let me help your baby, and your baby from now on will be my baby."

It took me nine days to get the drug and send it to her. It was embargoed. We couldn't send the drug directly from America to Iran. I found somebody in Europe. I bought a ticket for someone to take it to Iran. And when I was assured she had the drug, then I flew to Africa to do the oil deal with the head of state.

I flew from London to Africa, and when I arrived at the President's mansion, he was sitting and having barbecue chicken with one of his girlfriends.

I sat down and he said, "Good afternoon, Kiani." I replied, "Good afternoon, Chief; please forgive me. I know you were waiting for me for the last ten days, but I had a family problem. I hope you'll forgive me."

The President told one of his generals, "This gentleman is not allowed to leave my country without my permission." I said, "Mr. President, am I under arrest?" He said, "Yes, sir, I'm going to teach you a lesson. You do not keep the President of this country waiting for ten days." I knew I wasn't real*ly* under arrest, but the ten-day delay certainly irritated him.

The President asked one of the officers to bring me a shot of whiskey.

Cell phone rings at the *worst possible time!*

I thought I had switched off my cell phone, but that day I forgot. As the President was sitting there like a tiger, angry with me, my cell phone started ringing. I said, "I'm sorry, Mr. President. I do apologize. I forgot to turn it off."

He said, "Answer your phone." I said, "Mr. President, I will pick up the message later." He said, "No, answer your phone!"

I answered my phone. It was the woman from Iran, the mother of the baby. She was crying again. I said, "Now why are you crying? You received the drug last night." And she said, "Yes, I have the drug. I took it to my baby's doctor this morning, and he told me it's not good for my baby. It doesn't work on this particular leukemia."

I said, "Please, give me two or three hours. I'll call you back. Don't cry, please. The same God who brought us together will handle this. Don't cry."

And I switched off my cell phone and put it away. And the President said, "What was that?" I said, "Mr. President, that was a personal call." He said, "That phone call changed your face. What happened to you?" I said, "It's a private matter. Would you please leave it alone?" And he said, "No,

I want to know!"

I was already in trouble with him, and I didn't want to lose his friendship and his business. So I told the President the whole story.

He got up, hugged me, and he started kissing me. And he said, "Kiani, at least one or two people every week come to my mansion to request consideration for timber, gold mining, copper mining, everything. But I don't invite them to sit here in my house next to my girlfriend and drink with me. And thanks to my God, I was right about you. You're my man. I'm sorry if I was not polite with you. Now, what are you going to do?"

I said, "I don't know." He said, "Would you allow me to help you?" I said, "No, Mr. President. I started this myself. I want to finish it myself. And God is great. He will help." He said, "Fine, what are you going to do?" I said, "I don't know. My hands are full, and I have to call the doctor."

The President handed me his satellite phone and told me to use it.

"Only one doctor in the world can save this little girl"

I called the doctor. Amazingly, he picked up the phone on the first ring. I asked him for advice, explaining that the drug doesn't work on the baby. He said, "I'm sorry, I cannot do anything any more." I begged him to show me a way. And he told me he knew of only one doctor in the world who could save this baby. I said, "Okay. Give me the name." And he gave me the name and telephone number of Ferre Akbarpour, M.D., in Huntington Beach, California.

And it took me ten days to be able to talk to her.

When I called her, she was in Chicago delivering a lecture. She said, "Mr. Kiani, I know for the last several days you have asked me to talk to you, but I'm sorry. I'm a busy doctor and was not able to talk to you. But I promise you I'll do anything I can for your daughter." I said, "Doctor, she's not my daughter. I want to be her sponsor. I want to buy a drug for her."

Dr. Ferre said, "Wow! I thought people like you didn't exist in this life anymore." I said, "No, Doctor, there are millions. We just don't know them."

It was love at first sight

Four weeks later I was on a plane to meet Dr. Ferre in person for the first time. I arrived here in Huntington Beach with a ring in my pocket. I proposed marriage immediately. She said yes.

I put the ring on her finger, and we got married on the first night. And here I am.

I walked away from all those million dollar deals, oil projects, gas projects — everything. I said goodbye to all those kings and presidents, money and business and millions of dollars.

I came here, and now I'm the chairman of this clinic.

My wife treated the little Iranian girl by long distance. She sent her the finest nutritional supplements money can buy and was in close communication with the girl's oncologist. The oncologist was amazed at the girl's recovery. He called Dr. Ferre and said, "What I see with this girl I have never seen it in my entire life at work. I'm really interested in your work. I'd love to work with you closely, and I'd love to send you patients."

The little girl's mother sent us her pictures, letters, and paintings. She was always thanking us.

Just a few years ago this clinic had only a few hundred patients. Now we have 5,000 patients. We were chosen by the American Medical Review as a symbol of an alternative treatment center in the United States of America. They made a film of our clinic, and that film will be broadcast in 172 countries in seven different languages.

Most religions teach that in the next life there is a hell and a paradise. I believe I'm in paradise right now. We're treating people. We're helping people who have no hope.

I'm in paradise because at this clinic we're saving lives.

Contact information:

Dr. Iraj Kiani, Ph.D., Clinic Chairman
The Orange County Immune Institute
Pacifica Tower
18800 Delaware Street, Suite 900
Huntington Beach, CA 92648
Phone: 714-842-1777
Email: drferre@drferre.com
Website: www.drferre.com

Chapter Seven

The Hippocrates Health Institute: Where people go to "reset" their health

The Hippocrates Health Institute is named after Hippocrates, the Father of Medicine, who once said, "Let food be thy medicine and medicine be thy food."

The Hippocrates Health Institute is founded on this belief: "that a vegan, living, enzyme-rich diet – complemented by exercise, positive thinking and non-invasive therapies – is integral to optimum health."

My tour of this legendary health clinic/spa was different from my other clinic tours. Usually I'm the only one taking the tour, and sometimes I have a colleague or two with me for a tour. But at Hippocrates I was one of about two dozen people who took the tour, which the clinic offers weekly.

As an added bonus, the tour included lunch from the clinic's fabulous cafeteria. Those who take the tour are eligible for a discount if they decide to sign up for the three-week program.

Hippocrates is located on the grounds of a former horse ranch in West Palm Beach, Florida. The clinic still uses some of the original structures but has transformed the grounds into a state-of-the-art health spa in a subtropical paradise with winding paths, mature trees, meditation gardens, pools, and abundant amenities. Sculptures and statues enhance the grounds.

Cancer patients go to Hippocrates to recover their health, but many other people go there, too. Some seek a natural remedy for an ailment. Stressed out executives and others seek a health tune-up. And many go there just to detoxify and rejuvenate themselves. Some newlywed couples even go to Hippocrates for their honeymoon. For many, it's a life-transforming experience.

The Hippocrates Health Institute isn't an out-patient clinic. It's an in-patient clinic with doctors and nurses on staff. But it's more like a luxury health spa, in some ways similar to the spectacular Sanoviv health resort in Rosarito, Mexico.

A patient may go through the three-week program at Hippocrates with a companion, but the staff regards everyone as a guest, and the patient's companion goes through the program, too. At most clinics, the patient's companion pays a token amount for staying with the patient. But at Hippocrates the cost is the same for each because the companion gets the same rejuvenating and detoxifying health benefits as the patient.

The three-week program starts on Sunday, and one can start on *any* Sunday.

Each guest at Hippocrates meets with a nurse and doctor and starts with blood work. Then the medical team creates a *customized* protocol for the guest, which may include about 30 hours a week of classes and lectures, including exercise classes, nutritional classes, food preparation classes, classes on how to grow wheat grass and how to juice, and so on. Yoga and meditation classes are held in a large yurt – a Mongolian-style round tent with an open sun roof/sky light. Massage therapists use the mini-yurts, which are air conditioned.

When the weather is pleasant – as it often is in West Palm Beach – some classes are held outside in a grass-roofed open shelter.

Exercise recommendations are customized for each guest. Hippocrates has built a beautiful fitness center with state-of-the-art equipment. There are exercise classes for all guests of all levels, including classes that take place in one of the pools. Rebounding (bouncing gently on a mini-trampoline) is encouraged, and there's something for everybody because Hippocrates recognizes that the body needs exercise to be healthy. Because of the size of the property, 650 acres, bicycles are also available.

Unlike conventional doctors who focus only on the body, Hippocrates recognizes *three* aspects of health: body, mind, and spirit. Because the guest's emotional and mental state can affect health, the clinic provides meditation and psychotherapy. Massage therapy at the clinic promotes not only relaxation but also lymphatic movement, which is essential for detoxification. The clinic also offers colonic hydrotherapy as a detoxification strategy.

Cholesterol dropped 83 points in three weeks!

At the end of the three-week program, each guest gets more blood work to compare to the blood tests performed at the beginning of the stay. The improvement encourages and sometimes astounds the guest.

For example, our tour guide, Sheila, told us her LDL "bad" cholesterol dropped 83 points *in just three weeks*! Many guests are able to get off their medications, amazed at how quickly the body bounces back to health when you give it exactly what it needs.

The Tranquility Room features a wide variety of therapies and devices, including pulsed magnetic therapy, a bed that rocks you back and forth to move lymph, a laser device that boosts the immune system and helps move heavy metals out of the body, a bed with massage devices that go up and down your back, and a device you stand on while it vibrates, which many find relaxing.

For cancer patients, Hippocrates can be a life-changing experience. The lifestyle choices and skills learned at Hippocrates can become a blueprint for long-term healthy, cancer-free living. On the other hand, three weeks at Hippocrates will do no long-term good for the cancer patient who returns to a high sugar, fast-food/microwaved diet upon returning home.

Hippocrates provides specialized therapies for cancer patients, such as vitamin therapy by IV. This therapy also benefits guests who have digestive problems.

"Nobody goes hungry here"

The lunch at Hippocrates was wonderful – unbelievably flavorful and satisfying – much better than I expected from a vegan cafeteria! Our tour guide said, "Nobody goes hungry here. People are always surprised that they're not hungry."

When the tour guide took us inside the wheatgrass room, she encouraged us to take deep breaths because there's 30 percent more oxygen in the room than outside! She also said that deep breathing helps calm the nervous system and move lymph.

Hippocrates teaches guests how to juice their own wheatgrass, and the guests take responsibility for making their own – a task the juicing machines make simple. Guests drink two ounces of wheatgrass three times a day – a tiny amount of densely packed nutritional liquid that's said to be equivalent to 10 pounds of vegetables. Guests also juice various kinds of sprouts – buckwheat, sweet pea, and so on – which are loaded with protein.

Hippocrates also teaches guests how to grow their own wheatgrass at home, so they can continue drinking wheatgrass juice as a long-term habit. Only a small space is required to grow enough of this life-giving plant.

One unusual feature at Hippocrates is the foot reflexology stream, which is similar to the "barefoot park" next to a health clinic I once visited in Germany's Black Forest. Hippocrates encourages its guests to walk barefoot on the smooth rocks in the stream, an exercise that massages the acupuncture points on the soles of the feet. After the tour I went back to the stream, removed my sandals, and walked the foot reflexology stream twice.

Chlorine-free pools are ozone purified!

Hippocrates encourages guests to use the pools daily. Their pools are chlorine-free – a huge benefit. The pools are purified by ozone, an expensive method that's far superior to chlorine.

One pool is for water aerobics and swimming laps. Other pools are for relaxation. One pool contains mineralized salt water, a source of health benefits to those who soak in it. And there's also a cold plunge containing water at 55 degrees Fahrenheit for guests who want to cool off after sweating in one of the infrared saunas.

These infrared saunas, which are found all over Hippocrates, boost the immune system, assist the kidneys, and help detoxify through the skin. Our tour guide said the infrared sauna is amazing for injuries, for joints, for aches and pains, for the skin, and for collagen. Following the sauna with a cold water plunge improves circulation by moving blood from the body's extremities to the core.

Though Hippocrates is an in-patient clinic/health resort, our tour guide said Hippocrates does offer a one-day class every six weeks on kitchen techniques, food preparation, and how to grow wheatgrass. The class, which lasts about five hours and includes lunch, costs $49. She described it as "a fun day."

The basic cost of the program at Hippocrates is $7,500 for three weeks. If a patient brings a companion, the cost is $15,000 for both. This is a reasonable price for an impressive, world-class facility.

In fact, it's dirt cheap compared to conventional cancer treatment, which will hit six figures so fast it will make your head spin. The most ineffective treatments for cancer are the most expensive, such as harsh, poisonous chemotherapy drugs that can cost $10,000 a month or more. The most effective treatments are inexpensive.

Three weeks at Hippocrates can set the cancer patient on the path to health and could also change the patient's companion's life as well. The Hippocrates website features testimonials about a wide variety of degenerative health problems including brain cancer, thyroid cancer, and breast cancer.

Contact information:

Hippocrates Health Institute
1465 Skees Rd
West Palm Beach, FL 33411
Phone: 888-228-1755
Website: www.HippocratesInst.org

Chapter Eight

The doctor whose patient remarked, "I had no idea this kind of health care existed"

It's remarkable that Reno, Nevada, has *two* outstanding alternative cancer clinics. After interviewing Dr. James Forsythe at his Century Wellness Clinic, I walked over to the nearby Reno Integrative Medical Center where I interviewed Dr. Robert A. Eslinger, D.O., H.M.D.

Besides being an osteopathic doctor, Dr. Eslinger is also a homeopathic doctor. His approach to cancer treatment is similar to that of Dr. Forsythe, who was on the staff of Reno Integrative Medical Center until he left in 2002 to found his own clinic.

Cancer patients from all over North America travel to the Reno Integrative Medical Center, which has an impressive track record at whipping even the most difficult and stubborn cases of cancer.

In a moment I'll describe the Center's treatment methods. But first let me give you some true stories of terminal patients who got rid of their cancer at the Center.

71-year-old boasts the energy of a 40-year-old!

First I want you to hear 71-year-old Joe L. tell his story – in his own words. He came to Reno with advanced cancers of the lung and pancreas after conventional doctors had given up on him.

Joe says, "For three weeks at Reno Integrative Medical Center, I was treated for cancer, taught what to eat and what not to eat. I went home and made some major lifestyle changes. I returned to Reno later for additional treatments and training. I learned to monitor and build my body's immune system to maintain lasting health.

"I have also learned to handle stress in a more productive way.

"Today, I am free of cancer, without the trauma of chemotherapy or radiation. My energy and stamina have returned to that of a 40-year-old man, (not bad for a 71-year-old!)

"Reno Integrative Medical Center combined the best of God's natural remedies with solid science to restore me to optimal health. Without reservation, I highly recommend Reno Integrative Medical Center for anyone who wants to be free of cancer and live life to the fullest!"

Breast cancer patient says NO to poisonous treatments

When Patty A. got breast cancer, she knew her doctor would recommend chemo and radiation. But at least the doctor was honest enough to admit that even with the most aggressive chemo and radiation, the cancer would probably come right back.

Such honesty is refreshing but rare.

Fortunately, Patty heard about the Reno Integrative Medical Center. She says, "It just made so much more sense to me. I have never regretted that decision I made because it took me down the path of healing that only made my body stronger without any ill effects.

"I reported for 3 weeks of 'boot camp' at the Reno Integrative Medical Center. You can be sure the doctors and staff leave 'no stone unturned' when you go there for treatment. I was busy every day 'getting well.' I was impressed with Dr. Bob and the multiple tools to assess the status of the body's internal terrain.

"A family member of mine accompanied me every day to the clinic and was with me for a follow-up visit. Her response to this experience was, 'I had no idea this form of health care existed, it's absolutely amazing.'

"I was told to expect the cancerous lymph nodes to start shrinking and eventually go back to normal. And that is exactly what has happened. I can barely feel the affected lymph node in my neck. I thank God and the universe every day for everyone at Reno Integrative Medical Center. They are true healers."

"You can laugh about your cancer because there's hope!"

In November 2004 another patient, Dorothy H., was diagnosed with Stage Four colorectal cancer. Here's what she says about her experience at the Reno Integrative Medical Center:

"The doctors, nurses and staff are wonderful. They are loving, kind, encouraging, and treat everyone as if they are the only one there.

"The atmosphere is bright and cheery. You meet new friends and share with each other. It is a place where you can even laugh about the cancer because there is hope. It's not a scary place, but one that brings peace, and the treatments aren't painful. The whole staff has a positive cheerful attitude.

"There is a lot of laughter, too, which one needs during this time.

"I know the reason I bounced back so fast is because I chose not to do chemo or radiation. If you find out you have cancer, please, I beg you to go to the Reno Integrative Medical Center and talk to the doctors before you decide to do the traditional method. The doctors are upfront and honest and will let you know what is best for you.

"I can't say enough for the center. They saved my life. I should be home with the Lord, but He used that treatment to spare me for a little longer."

Jonna's doctor gave up on her pancreatic cancer

Jonna W. was diagnosed with a neuroendocrine tumor in the pancreas. Her doctor explained that surgery, chemo, and radiation were not treatment options for her cancer. She replied that she didn't want to go that route anyway because she wanted to do alternative medicine.

Her doctor did something that conventional doctors seldom do: He encouraged her to find an alternative because conventional medicine had nothing to offer her.

Jonna already knew about the Reno Integrative Medical Center because that's where her aunt had gone for treatment. Here's what Jonna says about her treatment at the Center:

"I made an appointment which was the beginning of a wonderful healing experience. The staff has been so helpful and caring. The positive energy is overwhelming. The practitioners have seen me through many problems, and they have found a cure or solution to almost all.

"My cancer is receding. All in all, I believe Reno Integrative Medical Center is 'the place' for cancer treatment from knowledgeable, caring and truly wonderful people."

Agent Orange victim finds cure for his cancer

Doctors diagnosed Vietnam veteran John S. with prostate cancer. The prognosis was poor. The doctors told him that even with surgery or radiation, he'd need a miracle to survive. He didn't like that message, so he sought a second opinion and even a third one.

But all the doctors said the same. His prostate cancer was terminal.

John resigned himself to his "inevitable" fate. But then he heard about the Reno Integrative Medical Center. With nothing to lose, he scheduled an appointment.

John says, "After consultation, I was put on an immune boosting protocol to fight my cancer.

After a year and a half my cancerous tumor started shrinking and today, almost four years from my original diagnosis, I am healthy and happy with no symptoms of the disease. I continue to take my supplements and can only thank the wonderful caring staff at the clinic. The staff is always pleasant and takes care of my needs, whether it is on one of my once-every-six-month visits or just quickly getting my supplements sent to me in a day or so.

"I contracted my cancer from a tour in Vietnam and from Agent Orange. I have lost seven other platoon mates from Agent Orange cancers. I only wish my disease would have attacked me sooner so that I might have been in a position to talk to them about Reno Integrative Medical Center. Unfortunately, all of them had passed away before I knew about my illness or alternative treatments available."

Uterine cancer patient's immune system saves her

Judy W. underwent harsh conventional treatments for her uterine cancer, including radiation five days a week for five weeks.

She says, "This brought my immune system so low, I knew I had to do something more to build my immune system and prevent a recurrence of cancer. Because of my sister's success 25 years ago in a similar program, I went to the Reno Integrative Medical Center. I had a live blood cell test, which showed an extremely low immune system.

"After a lengthy visit with the doctor, I started a three week course of daily IV treatment. I also started a program of supplements and was given a list of foods to avoid.

"At the end of three weeks, I felt I had made friends with the staff because of the loving care and concern I was shown. I return every three to six months to have my immune system monitored.

"In the past seven years, I have experienced only two slight colds, one sore throat, and no recurrence of cancer. I thank God I was led to this 'Haven of Hope.'"

How Dr. Eslinger defeats cancer

A new cancer patient at Reno Integrative Medical Center gets a two-day evaluation. Each patient spends an hour-and-a-half to two hours with a doctor.

The doctor does a thorough examination, going over the patient's records and health history. He pulls everything together to come up with an individual treatment plan.

The initial evaluation also includes two crucial tests: a 12-hour urine test to detect any heavy metal toxicity and a full-mouth X-ray to determine whether a dental problem might be the cause of the cancer. If the dental exam reveals an infected root canal or infected jawbone, the patient is referred to a biological dentist (i.e. an "alternative" dentist) to fix the problem.

The clinic's goal is to get the body into a state where it can heal itself. If there are problems in the mouth, they must be fixed. If the body is carrying around a toxic load of heavy metals, detoxification is necessary.

The core of the treatment plan is a three-week "boot camp" that features an immune boosting system of IVs developed by the clinic's founder, the late Dr. Douglas Brodie. These IVs contain various substances including cesium, a natural mineral that goes right to the cancer cells and puts them in an alkaline state. (Cancer cells can't tolerate alkalinity. They thrive in acidity.)

Patients receive an intravenous treatment every day, Monday through Friday, for three weeks. Thus, the IV therapy consists of 15 treatments altogether. This can be completed within three weeks if the patient starts on a Monday; otherwise, the IV treatments would go into a fourth week.

The patient also goes through a detoxification program, which may include colonic hydrotherapy. Although colonic hydrotherapy isn't currently available on site, there are therapists nearby.

After the three-week "boot camp," one of the doctors coaches the patient by phone for the next three months. These phone calls are regularly scheduled long-distance "office visits."

Patients come back once a month during those

three months for a three-day follow-up, during which they have IVs each day and meet with a doctor.

Some patients do so well they don't have to come back every month. The doctor might say, "You don't have to come back every month. Why don't you come back in two or three months?" But other patients might need to come back in two or three weeks.

Unique twist on Insulin Potentiation Therapy

One of the most effective alternative cancer treatments is insulin potentiation therapy (IPT). This therapy uses the cancer cells' craving for sugar in a clever way.

The doctor gives the patient insulin to starve the cancer cells of sugar. And then, when the cancer cells are craving sugar, the doctor gives them some by IV – along with a low dose of chemotherapy. Because cancer cells take up sugar at a much higher rate than do healthy cells, cancer cells are killed by the chemo-sugar combination while healthy cells suffer little harm. IPT has a devastating effect on cancer, and the Reno Integrative Medical Center used it for several years.

But in recent years the clinic has given IPT a unique twist. Instead of giving the cancer cells low-dose chemo along with the sugar, the clinic now gives cesium with the sugar. Cesium, as mentioned earlier, is a natural mineral that goes right to cancer cells and puts them in an alkaline state.

For IPT, the clinic prefers cesium to chemotherapy because cesium isn't toxic.

Hidden cause of many cancers

The doctors at the Reno Integrative Medical Cancer do what few other clinics do today: they identify the emotional and psychological cause of cancer. The doctors ask the patients, "What was going on in your life before your body allowed this cancer to grow?"

And the doctors have found that just about every cancer patient has experienced some kind of emotional shock that weakened the body, allowing cancer to get a foothold. These emotional shocks include divorce, problems with children or grandchildren, or other situations that cause anger, hate, resentment, and bitterness to build up inside.

These resentments must be resolved to help the body heal. And the doctors are skilled at bringing about emotional healing while the other therapies give a big boost to physical healing.

The clinic firmly believes it's necessary to treat the *whole* patient, not just the body.

Dietary recommendations

Some cancer patients who come to the Reno Integrative Medical Center have been vegans all their lives. As you may know, a vegan is a *strict* vegetarian who eats no fish, eggs, or dairy foods.

One vegan came to the clinic in tears, saying, "I have cancer. I shouldn't have cancer!" How can this be? How can vegans who've been trying to eat healthy their whole lives get cancer?

When a vegan comes to the clinic with cancer, the doctors usually find that the problem is the patient's diet doesn't contain enough protein. For this reason, the clinic doesn't *strictly* recommend vegetarianism

If you're going to eat meat, the clinic recommends organic chicken. If you're going to eat beef, eat grass-fed organic beef. Be careful of fish because these days they frequently have high mercury levels. The fish's mercury content depends on where it was caught and how high up in the food chain it is. Carnivorous fish such as salmon, tuna and swordfish have the highest mercury levels

Each patient receives individual recommendations for diet.

The clinic highly recommends the Budwig protocol for cancer patients. This protocol, which mixes flax oil with cottage cheese, is named after the legendary Germany physician Johanna Budwig, M.D. Dr. Budwig wrote a book describing this remarkable protocol, which has helped countless cancer patients get well.

The clinic also recommends sitting in the sunshine to get some vitamin D. In addition, the clinic offers specialized forms of massage to relax the patient and give the patient more energy.

The clinic administrator told me, "People feel the difference when they walk through the door. We just love our patients. We go the second, third, and fourth mile for them. We try not to be 'clinical.' We try to be homey, as you can tell from the décor of the office. We just really care about our patients. When they leave following their three-week intensive, there are tears in their eyes because they've felt cared for and safe. And this is a place of hope.

"Our doctors are just amazing. People have come out of their offices after spending close to two hours with the doctor, with tears in their eyes, saying, 'That's the first time I've ever had a doctor really listen to me' or 'That doctor just told me my whole life. How did he know that?' Just knowing what questions to ask is a gift. Our doctors are gifted men."

My interview with Dr. Eslinger

During my first visit to the Reno Integrative Medical Center in 2008, the doctors were so busy with patients it wasn't possible for me to interview them. During my 2013 visit, however, Dr. Eslinger sat down with me for an interview.

Dr. Eslinger uses laetrile – a natural cancer-killing substance that American doctors are forbidden to use in all but a few states. But he never gets hassled for using laetrile because he's licensed to do so under Nevada's homeopathic board.

He orders it from Mexico and has it delivered to his clinic for his patients. His patients can also order it from Mexico and have it delivered to their homes wherever they live. The one thing Dr. Eslinger can't do with laetrile is to ship it from Nevada across states lines. If he did that, he says he would go to jail for violating interstate commerce regulations.

How to take laetrile at home to prevent cancer

One natural substance that's high in laetrile is apricot seed. Dr. Eslinger said, "Apricot seeds are OK as a preventative, but they taste terrible." I disagree with Dr. Eslinger about the taste. I really like their bitter almond flavor, which tastes like almond extract.

But Dr. Eslinger prefers delivering laetrile by IV or in tablets to be taken orally, because the amount of laetrile in apricot seeds can vary. He said a preventative dose of laetrile is about six to nine apricot seeds chewed and swallowed – or one gram of laetrile in tablet form.

He told us cancer patients at home can take up to nine grams of laetrile in tablet form each day, but patients have different tolerances, and some patients may not be able to handle nine grams a day. In short, "one size doesn't fit all," and patients should only take the amount of laetrile their bodies can tolerate. (Nausea is a sign to back off and take less.)

Dr. Eslinger has also been using a homeopathic substance called salicinium for over a year with impressive results. He uses salicinium not only in IVs but also in IPT treatments. When his patients go home after the three week "cancer boot camp," he gives them a home protocol which includes oral salicinium.

This cancer therapy can also knock out shingles in two days

Ultraviolet blood irradiation (UBI) is another therapy that impresses Dr. Eslinger. UBI involves withdrawing a small amount of the patient's blood, exposing it to ultraviolet light, and returning it to the patient's body.

This therapy is completely harmless and nontoxic, but incredibly powerful. Though Dr. Eslinger doesn't have cancer, he treats himself with this therapy for the health boost it gives him.

UBI is so powerful it can even knock out shingles in two days. It doesn't destroy cancer cells circulating in the blood, but causes them to shed the protein coat that hides them from the immune system. When the stripped cancer cells are injected back into the patient's body, the immune system's cells can now "see" them, learn to identify them and kill them.

Dr. Eslinger administers IPT to a patient twice a week – not every day because it's stressful to lower the patient's blood sugar. He likes to perform UBI on the same day, right after IPT treatment, for the "one-two punch."

A factor that adds to his clinic's success rate, said Dr. Eslinger, is di-chloral acetate (DCA). The scientific explanation of how DCA works is involved, but to keep it simple, the doctor explained that DCA reactivates "apoptosis" (natural, programmed cell death) in cancer cells so that these cells die at the end of their normal life cycle. Healthy cells die naturally after dividing about 60 times, but cancer cells don't, making them virtually immortal unless the patient receives a treatment of some kind to help induce apoptosis.

"We've been using DCA since last fall, and it's very promising. We give patients DCA in capsule form on Monday, Wednesday, and Friday."

In addition, at the time of our interview Dr. Eslinger had put 30 patients on a compound called GcMAF obtained from a lab in Belgium. After about 10 months of the treatment, he was seeing "really good results." The "MAF" in GcMAF stands for "macrophage activating factor." Macrophages are a key part of the immune system. Like PacMan, they gobble up microbes and digest foreign matter you don't want in your body.

"But I never get sick – how did I get cancer?"

Some patients who consider themselves pretty healthy are shocked when they are told they have cancer. They tell Dr. Eslinger, "I never get the flu. I never get pneumonia. I never get sick. How did I get cancer?"

He tells them, "You can have a strong immune system and still get cancer if the cancer can find a clever way to hide from your immune system. It does this by secreting an enzyme. What the GcMAF compound does is enable the macrophages and T cells [another type of immune system cell] to neutralize this enzyme. Then the immune system can recognize the cancer cells as abnormal and attack them."

Dr. Eslinger reports a success rate of 60 to 70 percent for tough cancers

Dr. Eslinger told me, "An additional therapy we do – maybe no one else is doing this – is prolotherapy."

In prolotherapy, he obtains platelet rich plasma (PRP) from the patient's own blood and spins it in a centrifuge. Spinning the PRP separates it into layers. Dr. Eslinger draws off the thin layer because that's where he finds the T-cell rich plasma (TCRP). He isolates the thin layer and incubates it overnight at 102 degrees Fahrenheit, which is a fever temperature. This stimulates the T-cells to produce heat shock proteins, cytokines, which the T-cells can use to kill cancer cells. Then he re-injects the T-cells back into the patient.

Dr. Eslinger said, "It's just the patient's own cells, so there's never a bad reaction. We give the TCRP in one arm and the GcMAF in the other arm. I put our success rate somewhere between 60 and 70 percent right now – a lot higher than the 2.1 percent success rate of conventional cancer doctors when treating late-stage cancers. We use non-toxic therapies, yet we see tumors shrinking up."

Starve the cancer, not the brain!

As for an anti-cancer eating plan, Dr. Eslinger recommends a ketogenic plan that's high in protein, high in healthy fats, and low in carbs. He told me, "Cancer cells require 18-times more sugar than normal cells because of their inefficient metabolism. So some patients think if they stop eating all forms of sugar cold turkey, they'll get rid of their cancer.

"But the brain needs sugar as much as it needs oxygen. You could kill yourself by dropping your blood sugar level to zero: you'd kill the cancer *and* yourself.

"With a ketogenic eating plan, however, your body starts generating ketone bodies. The brain and our normal cells have a metabolic pathway to flip ketone bodies and use them for energy. Cancer cells can't do that: they have to have sugar! That's why a ketogenic eating plan will feed your brain while starving cancer cells.

"While the cancer cells are starving, we can hit them with things like salicinium and laetrile. A combination of therapies is necessary. There's no silver bullet."

For detoxification, Dr. Eslinger says it's important that the drainage systems of the body be working efficiently. "When a tumor breaks down and disintegrates as a result of our therapies, it's all the more important to have the five main elimination pathways working properly: kidneys, bowel, liver, lungs, and skin.

"The liver is the biggest detoxifying organ in the body, and it also has to process all of the incoming nutrition. To support the liver we use milk thistle extract, a product called Livatrate, glutathione, and alpha lipoic acid – the last two administered by IV. [Livatrate is a liver tissue extract.]

"The lungs also help detoxify the body, which is why breaths smell differently. If someone has foul breath for more than a day or two, they don't need more Certs. They need a doctor.

"The skin has sweat glands, and each gland is like a miniature kidney. Our patients use the clinic's BioMat, which uses heated amethyst crystals to emit infrared rays."

The BioMat is similar in effect to an infrared sauna and promotes detoxification through the sweat glands. A BioMat costs about $1,500, and some patients buy one for home use.

Dr. Eslinger also uses a Chi machine – an amazing and inexpensive low tech device that creates a wave motion throughout the body. This promotes detoxification through lymphatic movement. Patients can buy a Chi machine for less than $200 for home use. It's about the size of a bread box.

How to bounce on a mini-trampoline the right way

Another way to promote lymphatic movement, Dr. Eslinger says, is by rebounding on a mini-trampoline. "Patients shouldn't try to get 'air' when they bounce." In other words, mild bouncing in which your feet never leave the mini-trampoline is better than vigorous jumping. He said, "Just jiggle instead of trying to 'get air.' Rebounding will increase your bone density because the body responds to pressure.

"Jumping rope also moves lymph. You can just get light hand weights and jump without a rope. Jiggling for five or 10 minutes a day is very beneficial. It doesn't have to be continuous. You can spread it out."

I asked Dr. Eslinger why conventional doctors don't accept alternative cancer treatments even though these treatments are so obviously better than conventional treatments.

He replied, "I maintain most doctors don't read the research because there are more and more studies coming out that challenge their beliefs. For example, there are studies on prayer that show that if a group is praying for a patient in the ICU, the outcome is better than for a patient who isn't prayed for. And you don't even have to know the person you're praying for.

"I've found that doctors will harp and harp about the studies: 'Where are the studies? Show me the double-blind placebo controlled studies.' And then when the study comes out, if it disagrees with what they already believe, they'll discount it.

"Here's another example. One of my most recent articles in a local magazine called *Healthy Beginnings* was about the proven dangers of mammography, which can cause cancer. Studies from England show the dangers. But these studies are discounted because many doctors still have monthly payments to make for their mammography machines.

How unethical doctors use patients as human guinea pigs

"Sometimes patients ask me about volunteering to be part of a clinical trial. I ask them, 'Do you know what "clinical trials" are?' And I explain that they're medical experiments. When the chemo fails and the radiation fails, the conventional doctor says, 'Well, we can get you into a clinical trial at UC Davis for a new chemo drug.' Where's the double blind study on that? It *is* the double blind study! And the patients who are in the placebo group won't get the experimental drug the other patients in the study get. They're treating patients like guinea pigs. They speak out of both sides of their mouth.

"Most conventional oncologists go through life with blinders on because they were taught 'You're getting the best medical education in the world. If something isn't taught here, it's not even worth looking into.' That's asinine.

"The first principle of the scientific method is that you *start with an open mind*. Well, that has gone right out the window because the vast majority of doctors I come across tell me, when they find out I'm doing alternative medicine, 'Oh. Alternative medicine? That stuff is quackery.' To me, an intelligent response would be, 'What is alternative medicine? Explain it to me.'

"I also tell my patients that they're physical/mental/emotional/spiritual/psychological beings. Conventional medicine treats only their physical aspect. Conventional doctors attempt to treat the mental aspect with drugs, and that's not working very well. They'll admit that stress can cause disease, but they don't do anything to address it – as if we're all born with drug deficiencies and need prescriptions to be made whole. It's gross insanity, and it's run by the Pharma industry interests.

Congress protects the drug racketeers

"Vioxx was the prescription drug that killed 100,000 people before they finally took it off the market. It was approved by the FDA. And then they found the secret memos proving that the drug company knew about the dangers before they submitted it to the FDA for approval. But these drug company officials were never held responsible for the 100,000 deaths. Instead, Congress passed a law saying that if one of your loved ones was killed by Vioxx, you can't sue the company because the product was approved by the FDA! That, to me, is criminal. And it's all to protect the Pharma industry interests.

"The homeopathic medical board gives me the freedom to do natural medicine. There are only three states in the country that license MDs and DOs to do natural medicine: Nevada, Arizona, and Connecticut."

Dr. Eslinger told me that some of his friends from high school are starting to retire. But he says, "I feel as if I'm just getting started. I'm passionate about what I do."

Cost of treatment

The initial two day evaluation normally costs a little over $1,000, sometimes less. Insurance may cover it.

The cost of the three-week "boot camp" is around $17,000, which includes lab draws, supplements, and time with the doctors. This is a reasonable price.

Where to stay

Because the Reno Integrative Medical Center is an outpatient clinic, patients from outside the area stay at a hotel or in an apartment. There are several excellent hotels within two or three miles of the clinic.

The clinic has arranged for a corporate rate with the Residence Inn, which gives patients a good deal for a room with a kitchenette. This is what Dr. Eslinger prefers for his patients because he says it can be hard to eat healthy at the casino hotels. Patients can buy healthy foods at the local Trader Joe's or Whole Foods during their stay.

Contact information

Dr. Robert A. Eslinger, D.O., H.M.D.
Reno Integrative Medical Center
6110 Plumas Street, Suite B Reno, NV 89519
Phone: 775-829-1009
Toll free: 800-994-1009
Fax: 775-829-9330
Website: www.renointegrative.com

Chapter Nine

How the grandmaster of energy medicine reverses "terminal" cancer

You've heard the adage, "Give a man a fish and he'll eat for a day. Teach him to fish and he'll eat for a lifetime." If you're looking for a doctor who will "teach you to fish" when it comes to your health, Dr. Lance Morris, N.M.D., of Tucson, Arizona, might be just the right doctor for you.

Dr. Morris told me, "Making people dependent on our clinics would be somewhat irresponsible and self-serving. If I'm really doing my job right, patients who come to me will get better and go home without having to make repeated trips back to our clinic. If they keep coming back to me too frequently, it means I'm failing them, or they're failing themselves, or we're not communicating."

Dr. Morris's personal story, which I'll tell in a moment, is amazing. So are his successes with cancer cases most doctors would consider hopeless.

For example, one of the most shocking cases Dr. Morris has ever seen in his career was a young man who came into his medical office with severe squamous-cell carcinoma. This cancer had taken over his left eye and was going into his brain. "His eye was protruding a couple of inches out. It was really scary," Dr. Morris told me.

This particular kind of cancer is dangerous, quick, and lethal. It's not to be confused with basal-cell carcinoma, which seldom kills anybody but only causes discolored spots on the skin.

The young man's conventional oncologist proposed surgery that would remove his eye plus half of his face, followed by chemo. But the oncologist offered no hope of healing even if he consented to this drastic measure. The oncologist told the young man he was going to die of his cancer but expected him to go along with the treatment plan because these treatments are what oncologists are good at. The patient said no.

So he had no surgery, no chemo, and no radiation – natural treatments only. And Dr. Morris's natural treatments saved his eye and his face. "That was amazing and remarkable – and pretty hard to do," says Dr. Morris, "and he lived for eight more years with a good quality of life."

Another patient came to Dr. Morris with pancreatic cancer, which most oncologists consider a death sentence. Although this patient underwent a major abdominal surgery called a "whipple," his doctor told him, "We're not going to stop the cancer, and we're not going to save you. Maybe chemo can give you another six months instead of three."

When the patient refused chemo, the oncologist blew his stack and read him the riot act: "Without chemo you'll be dead in 30 days" and other abusive threats along the same lines. The patient let the tirade go in one ear and out the other. Then he looked for an alternative, and found Dr. Morris.

Using natural therapies only, Dr. Morris helped this pancreatic cancer patient achieve a stable remission. Four years into this remission, the lead oncology doctor – the one who'd blown his stack at the patient for refusing chemo – came down with pancreatic cancer. You have to give this oncologist credit for practicing what he preached, because he did choose conventional treatment – and he was dead within 60 days. Dr. Morris's pancreatic cancer patient lived 12 years – quite a few bonus years, with a good quality of life.

Dr. Morris has noticed an ironic fact: more doctors are being diagnosed with their own specific medical specialty. He claims there's a direct relationship: images we visualize in our minds together with strong negative emotions like fear, anger, and sadness can lead to a disease process.

Adding weight to Dr. Morris's theory, America's leading brain surgeon, Dr. Samuel Hassenbusch from the famous M.D. Anderson cancer hospital in Houston, died at the age of 54. The cause of his death? The same deadly brain cancer he treated: glioblastoma. He had chosen conventional therapy.

Conventional doctors and celebrities sneak into Dr. Morris's clinic

But not all doctors choose conventional treatment when they get cancer. It's not uncommon for conventional oncologists to sneak into Dr. Morris's clinic or similar clinics when they get cancer.

Celebrities have also found their way to Dr. Morris's clinic. A billionaire celebrity once made an appointment to sneak his wife into the clinic at night after the clinic had closed. At the billionaire's request, Dr. Morris used a fictitious name for the wife, to preserve confidentiality in ordering lab tests. These tests helped Dr. Morris identify what was causing her cancer – a first step in treating it.

Unfortunately, the billionaire chose to disregard both the tests and the treatment options Dr. Morris offered, and pulled his wife out of the clinic. She died soon after that.

This lady's conventional doctors never suspected, or tested for, the condition Dr. Morris found with his tests. Specifically the lab tests demonstrated a level of plastic residue in the patient's body, as well as antibody levels many times higher than Dr. Morris had ever seen.

Dr. Morris says cancer and other degenerative diseases are often caused by environmental factors such as petroleum byproducts, plastics, synthetic chemicals, drugs, pesticides, herbicides, ionizing radiation, and radioactive isotopes. Cancer patients typically need serious detoxifying therapy. This is a theme at almost every alternative and integrative cancer clinic.

A conventional doctor who only treats symptoms of a disease and ignores the fundamental cause is doomed to failure. Dr. Morris says it's necessary to get at the cause. His naturopathic perspective of "nature cure" empowers a patient to assume direct personal responsibility in their own health care.

Could Dr. Morris have helped Ted Kennedy with his brain cancer?

A form of cancer that stumps conventional doctors is glioblastoma – a form of brain cancer that's often called "glio" for short. That's what killed Senator Ted Kennedy, who trusted his doctors and chose conventional treatment.

A physician whose wife had glioblastoma brought her to Dr. Morris. "Other doctors often send me the tough cases," Dr. Morris told me.

This glio patient had tried conventional cancer treatment unsuccessfully. Patients with this type of cancer often die in less than a year. Five-year survival is rare. Dr. Morris said, "A major problem with glio is brain swelling, which often causes grand mal seizures."

He relieved this patient's swelling with intravenous DMSO. Dr. Morris said, "We stabilized her and controlled her cancer for quite a few years – seven or eight. This placed her in the top one percent of patients with glio for length of survival."

I asked Dr. Morris to tell me his story. I wanted to know how he got into alternative medicine. His story is fascinating.

Born in 1954, he was the third of three children. His mother's first pregnancy was difficult and dangerous for her and her baby. Her second pregnancy was even more dangerous. That's when her doctor put his foot down and told her to cease and desist. At her doctor's insistence, her husband got a vasectomy.

His mother became pregnant after his dad's vasectomy!

After the vasectomy she became pregnant with Lance! Dr. Morris asked me, "Was my mother fooling around? Was I immaculately conceived?" I replied that I believe in the Immaculate Conception, but I suspected that his father's vasectomy had healed, restoring his fertility, and that his father was his true biological father. Dr. Morris smiled as he replied that that was indeed the case.

His parents were magnificent role models. They grew up during the depression in New York City. His father was Catholic, and his mother was Jewish. Their families disapproved of their relationship.

After eloping to the local courthouse they decided to take off on the adventure of a lifetime. They placed their canoe in the Hudson River and headed North. They continued into the Erie Canal system, through the Great Lakes and into Canada. They built a cabin to get through the first winter.

Over a period of two years, believe it or not, they eventually made it all the way to Alaska – by canoe! Their longest portage (the arduous task of carrying the canoe and equipment overland) was 50 miles. They settled on a tributary of the Yukon River called the Porcupine, North of the Arctic Circle.

They were two "crazy" white folk who lived in the middle of nowhere with a 120-mile-long trap line to tend, using a dogsled and dog team. The hardships they endured would beggar the imagination. They stuck together in a marriage that lasted over 50 years until his mom passed away.

Dr. Morris follows his parents' example of commitment and love. He's been married to his wife Maureen for 36 years: "Our marriage was tempered early on by some tough stuff. During the toughest times we stubbornly refused to call it quits."

Lance's childhood: "Doctors, doctors, doctors, drugs, drugs, drugs"

Because his mother's pregnancy was so hazardous, Lance was delivered by C-section prematurely. Preemies often didn't survive in those days, but his parents assured the doctors, "Yes, he will survive." The family set up an oxygen tent at home and took shifts attending to him 24/7. His two older sisters were responsible for the bulk of his care.

Dr. Morris said, "My sisters often regaled me with stories of how they had to rock me endlessly. Oh, for the want of a modern windup baby rocker!"

A major problem with preemies is weak lungs: young Lance grew up with severe asthma and bronchitis. His parents took him to the best clinics and doctors: "Doctors, doctors, doctors. Drugs, drugs, drugs." Nevertheless, he was continuously ill and experienced severe respiratory crises at least three or four times a year.

Dr. Morris's life changed during his freshman year of high school. He attended one of the top private high schools in America, Verde Valley School in Sedona, Arizona – a place of stunning natural beauty. Lance felt drawn toward a group of students who were the "movers and shakers" at the school. These students were concerned about serious issues, and they happened to be vegan. By contrast, Lance loved meat and potatoes and enjoyed drinking lots of milk.

Lance wanted to hang out with the vegans, and he discovered that the best time to hang out with them was at the meal table. He told them, "I need to hang out with you guys." One of them replied, "No problem, but you can't bring any animal-based food to our table. You have to eat what we eat." Lance really wanted to hang out with them, so he said, "O.K. I guess I could go along with that."

Lance discovers the cure to his asthma!

Three months later Lance woke up one morning and realized he was breathing without using his inhaler and without being stuffed up. He thought to himself, "I wonder if my chronic asthma, chronic bronchitis, and chronic respiratory infections requiring hospitalization had something to do with diet." By trial and error he discovered he had a massive allergy to milk!

Dr. Morris told me, "Milk is the number one

allergen on our planet! The dairy industry and doctors perpetuate the notion that milk is the perfect food – withhold it from a child, and the parent is negligent! But if you go to a daycare center, you'll see the kids sniffling, sneezing, hacking, dripping from the nose, getting ear infections, and taking antibiotic after antibiotic. Nine times out of 10 it's a dairy allergy.

Lance decided to experiment by going back on milk. Lo and behold, his symptoms returned. And when he quit drinking milk, his symptoms disappeared. He knew he had the answer.

Excited about his discovery, he informed his parents that he'd discovered the cure for his asthma. His doctors tried to tell him that he'd simply outgrown it. Lance replied to the doctors, "I haven't outgrown anything."

The problem with dairy, Dr. Morris told me, is the way milk is adulterated through Pasteurization and homogenization. In addition, conventional farmers give dairy cows growth regulators, hormones and antibiotics, and feed them GMO grains and residue animal parts, mostly from other cattle. Feeding cows an unnatural diet instead of grass and hay is a bad idea.

In college Lance met his future wife Maureen. After they got married, he asked her, "What am I going to do with my life?" She replied, "You're going into natural medicine." He said, "Really? You can make a career of that?"

He looked into medical schools but rejected them because they weren't teaching what he wanted to learn. As for chiropractic, it was too narrow to suit him. His wife encouraged him to look into naturopathy, and he discovered that Bastyr University in Seattle offered an intensive high-powered four-year graduate program in naturopathic medicine. He went through this program, and after graduation, he hung out his shingle and built his practice from scratch.

That's tough to do, but back then there was no other way.

Cancer Treatment Centers of America: A mixed bag

For a select few naturopaths, there's a much easier way to make a living these days, but Dr. Morris says the "easy way" requires naturopaths to surrender their principles in exchange for job security. He told me that the Cancer Treatment Centers of America (CTCA), which advertises heavily on TV, will hire naturopathic doctors right out of medical school and give them a good salary and benefits. The naturopaths must agree that chemo and radiation are essential to the patient's treatment plan, and they must subordinate themselves to the chemo and radiation doctors. As long as the patient at CTCA gets chemo and radiation, CTCA allows the patient to consult with a naturopath about nutritional supplements and other natural therapies.

Dr. Morris says this is an important first step: if patients are going to take chemo and radiation they should also get nutritional therapies *as part of standard care* to reduce side effects and give them a better chance at survival.

Dr. Morris said that Arizona has even established board certification for naturopathic oncology. At first, he thought this was a good idea. But now he sees that those who become board certified as naturopathic oncologists must subordinate to conventional doctors and go along with the conventional chemotherapy and radiation treatments. This is a compromise no naturopathic physician should have to make, Dr. Morris says.

How, then, does Dr. Morris cure cancers that stump conventional doctors?

Like many alternative doctors, Dr. Morris doesn't like the word "cure." He prefers the word "heal." But he certainly does help people get rid of their cancer or keep it under control. He specializes in cancer but not by design. He told me that happened by accident.

Like other naturopaths of his generation, Dr. Morris uses ozone, ultraviolet blood irradiation, Iscador (mistletoe extract), vitamin C, and other natural therapies including herbal tinctures that he individually blends for each particular patient.

"I do all that stuff," he told me, "and these things increase the quality and length of life *every time*. Are any of these things a cure? No. Absolutely not. Now, I've had patients who were told they'd be dead in three months who lived 20 years after coming to see me. Did I cure their cancer? No. I just helped them find a pathway to a better quality of life.

It's a mistake to focus only on the patient's body

"It's necessary to integrate the patient's mind, body, and spirit. You can treat the body with such things as high-dose vitamin C by IV, but vitamin C treats *only* the body. High dose vitamin C is a non-toxic form of chemotherapy that actually kills cancer cells. In naturopathic medicine, however, the doctor treats the whole patient: mind, body, and spirit.

"People are taught that disease is bad, that disease is the enemy, and that we must fight against the enemy and win – as if cancer treatment were a kind of war. Cancer is seen as this evil thing, and doctors use chemo and radiation to try to kill it. Alternative doctors use high dose vitamin C, which is also a form of chemotherapy – non-toxic, but chemo nonetheless. But consider this. In a war, there are no winners – ever.

"The idea that cancer is the enemy and that cancer treatment is a war is the wrong way to look at it. Instead of looking at disease as an evil enemy, it's better to look at it as an ally – a gift that gives us a window of opportunity to learn and grow in ways we never would've otherwise. I help my patients change their thinking and their lives. They change their environment. They change their eating plan. They never would've done that except for the cancer. It's part of our growing journey. I try to bring patients into a place of gratitude and service to others.

"The cancer patient who feels devastated and remains stuck in this negative emotional loop probably isn't going make it. Patients with a positive outlook who have confidence in themselves and in their doctor have a better chance of survival."

Like other Naturopaths, Dr. Morris uses high dose vitamin C because it's a powerful treatment for cancer. But he's particular about the vitamin C he gives his patients. He doesn't accept just any vitamin C. Most IV bags of vitamin C are corn-based. If the corn isn't organic, it's GMO (genetically modified). Vitamin C IVs are often GMO, and Dr. Morris says that's *not* acceptable. He says many doctors who should know better say it doesn't matter, but it does.

The patient got better but caused a "stink"

Dr. Morris adds DMSO or a similar agent to the IVs he administers to patients. He likes DMSO because it's a universal solvent that strengthens whatever it's mixed with. He says, "That's a no brainer. Why use vitamin C *without* the molecules that increase the effectiveness of the treatment? The only problem with DMSO is that it makes people stink like garlic. So what? The smell goes away in a day or two. We tell patients it's going to happen. We have a leukemia patient who's using DMSO, and he stinks for two days. He went to work, and his boss told him he stinks. His boss and co-workers laugh about it and put up with it."

Dr. Morris's unique treatment: Resonant Sound Therapy (RST)

A lot of what Dr. Morris does is different or special. One of his unique therapies is the bioenergetic healing modality he developed and now specializes in. He calls it Resonant Sound Therapy (RST). This therapy, which I'll describe in a moment, uses the principles of acupuncture to find and release the energy blockages in the patient's body, but without needles or any other equipment. Dr. Morris uses touch and sound only.

As you may know, physicians in ancient China held that that energy flows inside the body through certain pathways called meridians. These meridians end on the skin at acupuncture points. When the energy that's supposed to flow through a meridian is blocked, health becomes impaired. When the energy is unblocked, health improves.

Are acupuncture meridians *invisible* channels under the skin?

It's a known fact that acupuncture meridians exist and that energy flows through them. Acupuncture schools teach that meridians are *invisible* channels under the skin, but Dr. Morris suggests a different description. The meridians aren't invisible but physical: the meridians follow a path on the only part of the human body that's 100 percent contiguous (i.e., touching along a boundary): the fascial membrane.

Fascial membrane: You may be wondering, "What's that?" Take an egg, for example. As you know, a human egg at fertilization starts out as a single cell, but the membrane of that cell soon folds in on itself, creating two cells. The two cells divide again, and you have four cells, then eight, then 16, and so on, as the baby develops in the womb. The membrane creates compartments in which the various organs develop. Without the membrane folding in on itself as the cells divide, none of this would happen.

Consider this. If you remove the nucleus of a cell, it dies, right? Wrong! The cell without a nucleus is still good to go. It lives. It just can't replicate. But what happens when you remove the *membrane* around the cell? In that case it disintegrates because nothing is holding it together.

The fascial membrane is a thin connective tissue that surrounds every muscle and ligament in your body. It also surrounds every organ of your body, every blood vessel, every lymphatic duct, and even crosses the blood-brain barrier. The fascial membrane is the only part of your body that's connected everywhere.

This is so obvious that just about everyone overlooks it. Most doctors are so focused on the patient's organs, they ignore the membrane that makes the organs possible and holds them and everything else in place. Dr. Morris focuses like a laser beam on this overlooked and ignored membrane through which energy flows.

How did the ancient Chinese doctors find acupuncture points?

Dr. Morris says, "As I started to personally wake up to the perception of this membrane in my own body I started to discover a lot of amazing things that have direct therapeutic applications. Acupuncture teaches that there's this energy, Qi [pronounced "chee"], that flows through the body through acupuncture meridians. We know it exists. Part of its quality is that it's electromagnetic. We can even use a machine to pick up a positive/negative charge, and we can detect a differential when the machine is on an acupuncture point.

"How did the ancients find the acupuncture points? Today we struggle with the best equipment and technology to find and demonstrate the existence of these points and meridians. We know they're real. It's no longer speculative. It's a fact. So how did the ancients discover it? I started to find, by directly perceiving my own body, the acupuncture points and meridians. Using a combination of touch and vocal sound, which I developed into Resonant Sound Therapy, I started to discover how to find the meridians and acupuncture points in others.

"Why does putting a needle in an acupuncture point activate a meridian? What I've discovered is that acupuncture meridians are embedded in the fascial membrane from the surface of the skin all the way to the bone marrow: it's a multi-multi-multi-multi-layered sac. This energy, this Qi, this electromagnetic charge travels on the fascia.

"There are areas of focal concentration – acupuncture points – because of the way the membrane folds as it encapsulates the muscles, nerves, blood vessels, and organs. An acupuncture needle can bring Qi to the surface of the skin. The acupuncturist takes the needle and spins it or bobs it up and down. When he connects with the Qi, the Qi 'grabs' the needle. The acupuncturist can feel it. That's when he knows he has connected to the Qi.

"Just sticking a needle into someone at an acupuncture point doesn't do much unless the acupuncturist also does what's necessary to connect to the Qi. When the acupuncturist turns and twists the needle and bobs it up and down, he's actually *twisting the membrane, the fascia*, like a stocking, and that's what makes the connection.

"If I pull your sock, and it's tightly woven, I'm pulling the entire fabric of your sock. What I've discovered is how to connect to the membrane and activate the Qi without needles. With Resonant Sound Therapy, for example, I can touch your finger and affect your toe.

"The way we create imbalance in the body's energy is that we twist and torque the fascial membrane. Every physical injury – whether it's a bike accident, car accident, knifing, or shooting – distorts the fascial membrane. So do emotional injuries. So do viral, bacterial, fungal, or parasitic infections, not to mention exposure to toxins. As long as a bad memory or experience still has an emotional charge, the fascial membrane remains twisted and distorted."

Dr. Morris uses Resonant Sound Therapy to re-establish the patient's energetic equilibrium.

Dr. Morris's energy therapy requires no devices – just sound and touch

"The unwinding of the fascial membrane allows the body to heal itself from the inside out. Here's how it works: I give the patient a foundation tone with my own voice, and the patient matches it by making his own vocal tone. Then almost immediately I make a complex resonant vocal overtone, which produces harmonic resonance. When you hum, you can feel your chest vibrating. When you change the pitch, you can feel the vibration go up and down the body.

"Linking my voice to the patient's voice enables me to find by touch where the fascial membrane is tighter. I can feel it clearly when I put my hand on the patient. The sound frequency is the pitch. The amplitude is the volume. I modulate both frequency and amplitude during the therapy. When the twisted fascia release, then energy can flow without restriction, allowing the body to heal itself."

Along with Resonant Sound Therapy, Dr. Morris teaches his patients how to generate their energy afresh every day by teaching them Resonant Movement Meditation, which they can do when they get home.

"I teach them how to be grounded while making certain motions that resemble Qigong or Tai Chi," he explained. "The key is to be able to consciously feel the energy stream moving in the body. I can teach them to replicate the sensation of Qi on a daily basis as it moves through the body so that their symptoms are no longer a problem. It's easy and fun."

Dr. Morris says the best thing about Resonant Sound Therapy and Resonant Movement Meditation is that they require no equipment. Even if the government tried to outlaw nutritional supplements, acupuncture needles, and other products alternative doctors rely on, such draconian restrictions wouldn't affect these two therapies.

Why you won't find carpeting in Dr. Morris's clinic

Dr. Morris is absolutely convinced that grounding – being connected to the energy of the earth – is essential to health and well-being. He says most people are ungrounded and disconnected from this energy because of synthetic carpeting and rubber-soled shoes, and they're paying the price in their physical ailments.

You won't find any carpeting in Dr. Morris's clinic. Instead, you'll find ceramic tile over the concrete foundation. When patients take their IVs, Dr. Morris asks them to take off their shoes and make sure their feet are touching the tile. He wants them to be fully grounded while they receive potentially life-saving treatment for their cancer.

Of course, Dr. Morris acknowledges that rubber is a remarkable material that creates more cushioning and durability for our shoes. He doesn't advocate any fanatical or extremist approach to anything. Instead he advocates and teaches common sense and moderation in everything.

He says, "A reasonable question is: how much or how long can we wear rubber-soled shoes and still remain healthy and in balance in mind, body and spirit? Is fifteen minutes of daily grounding enough to compensate for the onslaught of daily unbalancing exposures? How about two hours? Remember not very long ago all humans on this planet were grounded 24/7.

An easy way to be grounded

"Sometimes a patient will say, 'I couldn't walk barefoot. There are cactuses out there.'" He urges such patients to clear a spot for grounding – or else wear moccasins with leather soles.

After interviewing Dr. Morris, I went on the Internet and bought a pair of deer-skin-lined, leather-soled moccasins, which I wear without socks. They're so darn comfortable they've become my favorite footwear. They feel like a pair of "gloves" for my feet. A finely crafted pair of leather-soled moccasins costs over $100 but is well worth the price.

Other patients tell Dr. Morris, "I can't give up my dairy" or "I can't give up my chicken." Dr. Morris replies, "You can't? And you have cancer?" Others say, "Now that I'm cured, I can go back to my cigarettes and alcohol." Dr. Morris replies, "Really?" Following the doctor's advice is wise.

Nothing succeeds like success

As you can see, Dr. Morris's ideas are a long way from mainstream. Some may scoff. But nothing succeeds like success, and his results are extraordinary.

To make sure nothing interferes with the flow of energy during the patients' IV treatments, Dr. Morris asks the patients to place their cell phone away from their body and to remove their watches, jewelry, and wedding bands. He says some patients comply with his request and others prefer not to. His philosophy is that you can lead a horse to water, but you can't make him drink. He does his best to point his patients in the right direction. The rest is up to the patients.

Dr. Morris told me, "When I do energy work, I don't want anything like a watch or jewelry to interfere with it. Most of us wear a wedding band 24/7. This is dangerous. It's a serious problem. Just take it off at night when you go to bed so the body can clear the energy. Otherwise it warps the energy field, which can promote disease."

Dr. Morris is convinced that modern devices such as microwave ovens and mobile phones can cause serious health problems. He does have an iPhone, but he avoids keeping it on his person and putting it up to his ear. Rather, he sets it down on his desk.

If he's at a restaurant, he'll set the mobile phone down on the table. He said people can avoid putting a cell phone to their ear by putting it on speaker mode or by using the "blue tube" (not to be confused with "blue tooth"). A blue tube accessory works like a stethoscope to conduct sound from the mobile phone through a hollow plastic tube into your ear canal. These are available from his office or website.

Unique twist on essential oils: taking them by IV

An unusual therapy Dr. Morris practically swears by is essential oils administered by IV. He told me, "When I started this therapy I was one of only two doctors in the world who's developed a protocol using intravenous essential oils. There's a tremendous amount of research in Europe about the clinical use of essential oils. These oils are incredibly powerful clinical substances, but the idea of using them *intravenously*? Wow! Unprecedented, unprecedented!

"Dr. Gary Young, the other doctor who uses intravenous oils, set up a clinic in Costa Rica. We both presented papers at a medical conference dedicated to the use of essential oils for cancer therapy. At the conference he said, 'To date, every single cancer patient that's ever walked through the door – regardless of the form or stage of the cancer – has left in remission. Every single one, using essential oils by IV.' It's a really exciting area."

If a patient is determined to use chemo, Dr. Morris recommends Insulin Potentiation Therapy (IPT). IPT does involve the use of chemotherapy, which Dr. Morris never uses in his own practice, although he will refer patients to integrative MDs who do.

IPT is a clever technique that tricks the cancer cells into letting their guard down so they can be killed off by low-dose chemo or another such treatment. In IPT a patient is given insulin to drive their blood sugar down. Then the patient receives an IV of dextrose/sugar mixed with a much lower concentration of chemotherapy than is used by regular oncologists. The cancer cells, which crave sugar, eagerly take the sugar *along with* a low dose of chemo that's less toxic but more effective.

If IPT is more effective and less toxic than chemo alone, then why isn't it the standard of care for all oncologists? The reason is because the drug companies make some of the biggest profits on chemo drugs. Some drugs cost $10,000 per injection. Insurance pays for it. It's insane.

How the drug racket cons desperate cancer patients

"The FDA in cahoots with drug companies has come up with a way to get around the $100 million it takes to get an orphan drug on the market: 'compassionate care' programs," Dr. Morris told me. "Orphan drugs" are those for which the market is too small to be worth spending the money to get the drug FDA-approved.

"When cancer patient Mary Smith has received chemo that didn't work, her doctor says, 'Mrs. Smith, we have this incredible offer for you. You can be part of a trial in a study for a new drug. Just sign here so you can be a part of it!' Mrs. Smith gets excited. There are only 100 people in the trial, and she 'gets' to be one of them. This is gross and unethical human experimentation. Usually everybody dies, but people are eager to sign up for it. It's crazy. And the FDA gives its stamp of approval."

In Dr. Morris's opinion, "Naturopaths are held to a higher standard than allopathic physicians (MDs and DOs).

"If someone is harmed under the care of a naturopath, the naturopath is toast! But MDs often cause harm and are held blameless.

"I'm a driven guy. And I'm doing a lot right now in my healing work and in my field. I want to teach." He has written a book, *The Edge and Beyond: A Journey for Personal Self-Discovery, Awakening, and Healing*. In the second edition of his book, which may be available by the time you read this, he made some changes to render it more user-friendly for the layperson. If you read this book, be sure to get the second edition.

Dr. Morris's dietary recommendations

Dr. Morris doesn't recommend one particular eating plan for everybody because he believes one size doesn't fit all. Rather, he makes individual recommendations for each patient. He posed an interesting question about diet: "If I were stranded on a desert island and had to pick six foods, what would I pick?" These are the six foods he mentioned, and the rationale behind his choices:

- Miso fermented soy. The only problem is that soy is often GMO, which should be avoided. Soy needs to be organic! And it must be unpasteurized. In restaurants it's often pasteurized. Believe it or not, a tablespoon of unpasteurized miso paste has more enzymes than a quart of carrot juice, and more lactobacilli and pro-biotic acidophilus than a quart of yogurt.
- Blue green algae – spirulina, chlorella, or duniella: one of nature's perfect foods. If you take blue green algae and add water and fiber you can live on it for the rest of your life with no nutritional deficiencies. Unfortunately it has no taste.
- Seaweed – a common part of the Japanese diet. Seaweeds are unparalleled in trace minerals, and trace mineral deficiencies are common.
- Brown rice: from a Macro-biotic perspective, brown rice is the most balanced of all foods – specifically balanced in terms of Yin and Yang. Again, Dr. Morris is not suggesting a clinical or medical preference for Macrobiotics. He is only honoring this among many food systems.
- "Pick a fruit."
- "Pick a vegetable."

Because Dr. Morris asked me to pick a fruit and a vegetable, I picked the mango and the Brussels sprout – though I'm not planning to be marooned on a desert island anytime soon. He approved.

Tucson:
A world class spa destination

Dr. Morris told me that the health spas in Tucson attract people from all over the world. The scenic Canyon Ranch spa provides its guests with organic high-end food, spa treatments, and a world-class experience.

A newer spa called Miraval is also world class. In any given week, the rich and famous can be found at these spas. I didn't visit either of those places when I was in Tucson, but I did buy a $25 day pass for the spectacular Marriott Omni Resort. I took full advantage of the pool, sauna, steam room, and cold plunge. The cold plunge was so cold it felt as if knives were stabbing my legs when I came out of it – just the way I like it.

Dr. Morris told me he definitely believes in the health benefits of cooling off in the cold plunge upon leaving a sauna. He said it's a tradition in Fairbanks, Alaska, where he grew up, to jump into a snowbank or into an icy river after coming out of a sauna. He said that early in the 20th century many spas offered water cures, and that these natural cures are starting to gain in popularity.

Cost of treatment, and where to stay

Dr. Morris's office is modest, and his overhead is low. His prices are reasonable. Each case is different, and the cost differs depending on which treatments the patient receives.

In Tucson there are hotel options to suit any budget. The clinic can recommend various options for lodging.

Contact information:

Dr. Lance Morris, N.M.D.
Wholistic Family Medicine
1601 N Tucson Blvd #37
Tucson, AZ 85716
Phone: 520-322-8122
Website: www.ResonantSoundTherapy.com

Chapter Ten

The prostate cancer specialist who helps men avoid unnecessary surgery

While sitting in the waiting room before my interview with Phranq Tamburri, N.M.D., I picked up the current issue of a medical publication featuring a front page article by Dr. Tamburri and read it. The article, "Prostate Cancer Update: Rethinking the Problem," was long and thorough. He certainly *has* rethought the problem!

At the end of the article there was a blurb about Dr. Tamburri that said: "He was resident and then chief resident, and eventually the first naturopathic physician to conduct rounds with Mayo Clinic urologists." That's impressive. The blurb also said he lectures on Austrian Economic vs. Keynesian theory, which I found interesting.

When we sat down for the interview in his office, I was going to ask him something about cancer, but I needed to ask him this other question before it slipped my mind. I interrupted my first question and said, "First let me ask you this. Are you a fan of the Austrian school, or are you a Keynes man?

He burst out laughing and wondered how I knew he was interested in that subject. Then he said, "I'm definitely an Austrian School man." His interest in the Austrian School of Economics is quite relevant to the story of how he decided to become a naturopathic doctor.

I asked him to tell me his story: how did he get into integrative medicine specializing in the prostate?

He was the science geek with Tourette's syndrome

Dr. Tamburri said he was a quiet kid and a science geek. He wanted to be a public speaker, but he had Tourette's syndrome. He stuttered and had all kinds of problems and, despite his desire, he didn't think he could do public speaking.

He started looking at medicine because it seemed like a good way to be a capitalist – to have a small business and work for himself. This idea dovetailed perfectly with his strong beliefs about economic freedom that he'd learned from the Austrian School.

He went to college in Japan and lived there for a while in a Buddhist monastery. For a while he also lived with a Japanese family. He says that's when his Tourette's syndrome was "the best it was" because of the Japanese diet and the nightly ritual of soaking in the ofuro (Japanese hot tub) outdoors, even in the cold of winter. As the guest, he was allowed to enter the nearly scalding hot water first, and then the members of the host family joined him for a good, relaxing soak.

Dr. Tamburri remarked, "You come out of the tub with red skin, and when snow hits it, no problem. They didn't have central heating, and they had the windows open with snow coming in. After the hot tub my mind was alert, and I crashed, had great dreams, and woke up alert. The Asian way of life is so beneficial in that respect."

His remarks about the ofuro reminded me of something one of the speakers at a Cancer Control

Convention said: "Getting a Japanese hot tub is the best money you'll ever spend!"

When Phranq came back from Japan, Bill Clinton occupied the White House and Hillarycare was being debated. That's when Phranq decided against becoming a doctor. He felt that Hillarycare or something similar was coming to America sooner or later, and he didn't want to take on a big debt to become a doctor only to be told what to do by a bunch of pencil pushers and bean counters.

To put his daily bread on the table he took a variety of jobs related to medicine. He got a taste of the "pharma industry" by working at Merck pharmaceuticals. He also did drug testing for the FDA. For a while he drove an ambulance as a paramedic.

He had to "scrub in" just like a surgeon

To further involve himself in the medical field, he joined a surgical team for organ transplant retrievals. Eventually he became the head of this team and was responsible for extracting eyes and cutting out hearts and other organs. Just like a surgeon, he had to scrub in next to the operating room. He got a similar job at a different lab where he was assigned cadavers that had been donated to science. Once again, he was cutting out hearts and other organs – this time for research.

In other words, he circled *around* being a doctor and did all these things without actually being a doctor.

Then came an event that changed the course of his life. He attended a lecture about ozone therapy, and the speaker mentioned a book by an ND. That struck him: an *ND*? What the heck is that, he wondered. He asked whether the speaker meant to say "MD," and he found out that an ND is a naturopathic doctor. He also discovered that a licensed ND is in every sense a physician who can prescribe not just herbs and vitamins but also drugs – just like an MD.

This discovery was a dream come true for Phranq. Because naturopathic doctors are licensed by only a handful of states, an ND is off the radar screen of federal agencies and regulators. He realized he could provide valuable services in a cash-only practice and be in business for himself.

So Phranq went to one of the leading naturopathic medical schools, got his degree, and started his practice as an ND. He has established a reputation among the well-informed as perhaps the leading prostate specialist in America. He remarks that a "holistic specialist" is an oxymoron – a contradiction in terms – because holistic doctors look at the three aspects that make up the whole patient: mind, body, spirit. Though he specializes in the prostate, he's careful not to lose sight of the big picture.

Many prostate cancer patients are surprised when Dr. Tamburri asks that the wives also be present for the consultation. He tells them that the wife is part of the team and needs to be included.

"I get to play in my sandbox with the MD's toys"

Dr. Tamburri chose to specialize in the prostate to help men avoid unnecessary prostate-removal surgery. He says, "The prostate specialty lets me use the full extent of my license. I can use things like Doppler ultrasound, which MDs use. I can play in my sandbox with the MD's toys. It's rewarding. When patients give you a hug at the end of the office visit, you know you're doing something right, and you're helping them."

And by the way, Dr. Tamburri told me, "If you only have space for one paragraph, say that I do Doppler ultrasound." Fortunately, I have no such limitations.

Is the prostate cancer like a poodle or a rabid dog?

Ironically, Dr. Tamburri usually doesn't *treat* prostate cancer at his clinic. That's not his specialty. He knows how to treat it, but so do a lot of other NDs and holistic MDs. These other NDs and MDs often refer their patients to Dr. Tamburri to *evaluate* how dangerous the cancer is.

Specifically, he answers questions like these: Is the prostate cancer like a poodle or a rabid dog? Is the problem benign prostate hyperplasia (BPH)? If so, what kind? Is it the kind that grows large or the kind that becomes dense? Is the problem prostatitis? Or is the problem all three: cancer, BPH, *and* prostatitis?

Dr. Tamburri is the only doctor I know of who specializes in answering these questions. He told me, "If there is a cancer, it's like a polar bear on an iceberg during a blizzard. The iceberg is BPH, and the blizzard is the prostatitis." It takes a rare skill to see what's really going on.

His unique niche is to determine how dangerous a prostate cancer is. After evaluating a patient's cancer, he gives the patient a comprehensive report and analysis, explains it to the patient thoroughly, and sends the patient back to his doctor for appropriate treatment.

If a patient with low-grade prostate cancer wasn't referred by another doctor, Dr. Tamburri can treat him, but if it's Stage Four prostate cancer he would refer the patient to another doctor in the clinic who specializes in difficult cases.

Dr. Tamburri doesn't treat late-stage prostate cancer because he says Stage Four is "a different animal." Late-stage or Stage Four cancer has spread from the original site in the prostate to other sites in the body.

He doesn't steal other doctors' patients or try to sell them supplements they can get from their own doctor. That's why so many NDs and MDs are happy to refer their patients to him.

He says, "I've been a professor of urology for about 12 years at the medical school. I know the treatments. I teach the doctors. They give me referrals. I help doctors figure out: What *are* you treating? Is the patient even a candidate for natural treatment? You have to know!"

He says the medical system has found it cheaper and less risky for legal liability to remove the prostate – even when it's not necessary.

Too many men lose the "prostate ping pong game"

Dr. Tamburri describes the debate about prostate cancer between conventional and alternative doctors as "the game of prostate ping pong, and the prostate is the ball." The surgeon tells the patient, "The PSA is elevated. You need a biopsy." Then the alternative doctor says, "The PSA isn't reliable. Don't get the biopsy because it'll spread the cancer all over, and then you'll die." These are two different views, but Dr. Tamburri understands both sides.

Some patients get the biopsy, and then the ping pong game continues. The surgeon says, "Let's take it out or fry it out or freeze it out or nuke it." The alternative doctor says, "Why do that? There are bad consequences to radical surgery or nuking. No one dies of prostate cancer. Just buy my supplements."

Dr. Tamburri poses some questions about this ping pong game. He asks, "Are surgeons helping the patient or their malpractice insurance or their personal finances? Alternative doctors have the best intentions, but do they know enough to recognize the most serious cases? They don't have the background of surgeons." He says many alternative treatments work well, but in some cases surgery is appropriate.

Because Dr. Tamburri is legally a full primary care physician (PCP), he has liability issues. He will tell a patient, "If you want me to make an educated assessment that might be contrary to what the allopaths would say, I need to know we're on the same page." He seeks to empower the patient. He wants the patient to understand all of the answers so he's not scared into surgery.

Dr. Tamburri asks, "Who will take the liability risk and say, 'I don't think there's a problem with this cancer'? That's a hard call to make, and that's what I do with all of the tools I use.

"My patients who choose surgery do it for the *right* reason. Surgery isn't always the end of the world, and natural medicine can't cure *everything.* Some men who believe their prostate surgery was unnecessary write books demonizing doctors. My patients – even those who chose surgery – aren't mad at me and still send me Christmas cards."

Hollywood producer's prostate was 10 times the normal size!

The main reason patients see Dr. Tamburri is to

get the 10- or 12-page report based on the Doppler ultrasound examination. He told me he relies on Doppler ultrasound because he can't evaluate a still photo. Doppler ultrasound gives him an entirely different picture of the prostate, allowing him to examine the prostate in real time in an interactive way, "like a video game."

"Basically," he explained to me, "you don't want to see any color." It's like Doppler radar for weather: if you're planning a picnic, you don't want to see color on the radar screen. He showed me a sample report.

Doppler ultrasound shows just about everything about the prostate, identifying the trouble spots in addition to information like the density and volume of the prostate. A normal volume is 20 to 30 ml. The largest prostate he has ever personally measured was an astounding 350 ml. It was the prostate of a Hollywood producer. After determining the volume, Dr. Tamburri looks for areas of disease.

He also does a genetic test, the PCA3 marker test. He says, "That's the most accurate lab test out there for positively predicting prostate cancer." He also does the traditional digital rectal exam "finger wave," which gives him a comprehensive understanding of the patient's prostate. When he palpates a "nuked" prostate – one that's been subjected to heavy doses of conventional treatments – he told me there's nothing to feel, no tone to the prostate: "It's like a physical silhouette – like a popped balloon."

He says that most surgeons are like the IRS: "They assume right off the bat that the patient is 'guilty' of having cancer – even though they know that most PSAs are elevated for non-cancerous reasons. But because they're worried about getting sued, they run down that path of ripping the prostate out. I go about it the opposite way. I look for what else could be causing an elevated PSA before I jump to the conclusion that it's cancer.

"Patients think I'm looking for cancer. Of course, I'm looking for it, but I want to know what else might be causing the PSA to go up. Some patients get flipped out over a PSA: to biopsy or not to biopsy, that is the question?"

Two questions Dr. Tamburri won't answer

There are two questions Dr. Tamburri won't answer. The first question is: "Do I have prostate cancer?" He says, "I can't legally diagnose cancer without a biopsy. If a patient has already been diagnosed, I can't legally tell him that he *doesn't* have cancer.

"Some people spend a lot of money on alternative treatment, and then they come to me and want me to tell them whether it's gone. If a patient has been diagnosed with prostate cancer, he'll never, ever be free of prostate cancer *legally*. He might actually be rid of the cancer, but he'll never be free of the prostate cancer diagnosis. If the PSA is under 4, does that mean the cancer is gone? Not necessarily. I have seen people with full blown cancer and a PSA of 1."

A patient might get another biopsy, but Dr. Tamburri says biopsies sometimes miss the presence of cancer.

The second question Dr. Tamburri doesn't answer on the first visit is what kind of treatments the patient should have. That's because just about all of the patients are already being treated by another doctor. The first visit may take two or three hours, and the main purpose of the visit is to find out *what* is being treated.

If the patient insists that Dr. Tamburri give him an herb or something right then and there, he replies, "If your cancer is so bad that you need an herb tonight, an herb isn't going to help you, and you should have it cut out!" He can refer a patient who needs or wants surgery to the Mayo Clinic in Phoenix.

Dr. Tamburri's approach to medicine is integrative. He says, "I know how allopaths think. I got in with the male urology guys. If I'm an alternative doctor, I have to know what I'm the alternative to. You have to know the other side. I understand both worlds. I can be a translator. I understand how the conventional doctor sees the case. I need to understand how the patient is being handled. I bring all of that experience to the patient's case. I get to know the patients well, and they fly back every six or 12 months."

Dr. Tamburri's "FOUR INFAMOUS QUESTIONS"

Dr. Tamburri makes a promise to his patients on their first visit that, at the end of the visit, they will have answers to what he calls the "four infamous questions." Here they are.

QUESTION ONE: "What is the chance that Dr. Tamburri thinks you have a reproducible prominent prostate cancer sequestered to the gland" (and not just an anomaly)?" In other words, "What's the chance that he thinks you have *real* cancer?"

QUESTION TWO: "If Dr. Tamburri think's there's a prominent cancer in your prostate, how aggressive does he think it is?"

Here's the thing about prostate cancer. It doesn't kill a man unless it escapes the prostate. Some patients want Dr. Tamburri to watch their prostate closely and then to alert them *right before the cancer escapes the prostate* so they can have it surgically removed. He says, "They're asking me to take a huge liability risk. I'll do that, but I want to make sure the patient is on the same page with me. Patients decide what's the comfort level for them. Do they have the money to return to my office once or twice a year? If the patient isn't willing to do the tests, then he's throwing liability on me. If he is willing to do the tests, he's going to be tied with me so that if I go off the bridge, the patient is coming with me."

QUESTION THREE: "If you have cancer but it's not a problem, or if you don't have cancer, why is your PSA so high?

Which of the "Three Stooges" is the culprit?

Dr. Tamburri says, "I can only handle three things: cancer, BPH, and prostatitis. Those are the three things that can make the PSA go up – like the Three Stooges, Larry, Moe, and Curly. Which *one* is making the PSA go up, or which *ones*? Sick glands beget cancer, and BPH or prostatitis can result in cancer.

QUESTION FOUR: "How does Dr. Tamburri track you?"

He says, "Patients have read on the Internet that the PSA is worthless. The medical system only wants to pay for one PSA test, and one test alone *is* a bad test. If you have multiple PSAs, you can do more with it. A guy came in here with a PSA of 3,400 and told me, 'My doctor was yelling at me to have my prostate taken out, but I read the PSA doesn't work!' I'm like, dude, we've gotta have a talk."

In his experience, any PSA over 10, in most cases, is a cancer. The highest PSA he has seen that wasn't a cancer was 32. He poses this question to his patients: "How do I track you if you don't trust the PSA? What are we going to use?" Using multiple tools and annual or semi-annual followup visits, he's able to track patients who want him to track them.

The veteran who had "prostzilla"

Oddly, some men have PSA-independent cancer. These cases might be caused by something like exposure to Agent Orange or DDT. One patient who'd been in places like Korea and Vietnam had what Dr. Tamburri calls "prostzilla." His whole prostate was like a rock, and all 12 cores were positive for cancer. But his PSA was only 2!

Dr. Tamburri explained, "Gleason scores indicating prostate cancer are numbered 6, 7, 8, 9, and 10. Ninety-nine times out of 100, the Gleason scores are six or seven. Black men sometimes get eight. Nines are horrible. Tens are beyond horrible. Once or twice a year I see a 10. It's like Bigfoot or the Loch Ness Monster. You hear about it but you're not likely to see it."

Prostate cancer patients who want to know how bad their cancer is would be hard pressed to find a more qualified doctor to make that determination than Dr. Tamburri. You can find him in Phoenix, Arizona, at the Longevity Medical Health Center, which he described as the oldest and largest private naturopathic clinic in the Southwest.

Contact information:

Dr. Phranq Tamburri, N.M.D.
The Longevity Medical Health Center
13832 N 32nd St, Suite #126
Phoenix, AZ 85032
602-493-2273
www.LongevityMedical.com

Chapter Eleven

The legendary doctor who harnessed his patients' mind power to whip "hopeless" cases of cancer

Dr. O. Carl Simonton, M.D., generously let me interview him by phone from his home in Malibu. Tragically, a few months later he choked to death while eating a meal at his home. Though Dr. Simonton is gone, the Simonton Cancer Center is still saving lives using the healing methods Dr. Simonton pioneered.

Dr. Simonton's most startling and revolutionary discovery about cancer treatment is this: Your beliefs influence your health — for better or for worse. In other words, your imagination can help heal you or it can make an illness worse. It can even kill you.

Dr. Simonton told me, "The impact of counseling on the course of cancer is solidly documented. Three randomized, controlled studies now prove that counseling doubles the expected survival time and improves the quality of life.

"With counseling, we see increased numbers of long-term survivors. And the 'side effects' of counseling are desirable. But there's a resistance to embrace new concepts. That's the problem."

Skeptic converts to believer

In fact, one skeptic, David Spiegel, M.D., a psychiatrist from Stanford University, did a study in 1989 to *disprove* the effectiveness of Dr. Simonton's counseling methods on cancer patients.

The results shocked Dr. Spiegel because *all* of the cancer patients in the control group were dead within 48 months of entering the study, but one-third of those in the other group — the cancer patients who got counseling — were still alive!

Those in the control group survived an average of 19 months; those who received counseling survived an average of 36 months.

The Spiegel study, published in the prestigious medical journal *The Lancet,* surprised the worldwide medical community. This study carries a lot of weight because Dr. Spiegel started out as a skeptic but couldn't ignore the facts. [Editor's note: Here's the reference for Dr. Spiegel's study: *Lancet* 1989; 2: 8668: 88891.]

Though Dr. Simonton's discovery is well established, most doctors today are still treating ONLY the body — as if the body were separate from the mind. That's a grave mistake because the mind and the body are one.

Dr. Simonton told me that doctors who treat the patient as if the patient's mind has NO role in the treatment process miss the big picture: they fail to see the mind as the single most powerful force for healing.

Dr. Simonton believed in treating the patient as a whole, instead of separating the mind and body. His methods have spread to holistic medical centers here and there throughout America. A few conventional doctors, too, are discovering and applying his ideas, but most conventional doctors treat only the body.

I asked Dr. Simonton if he could give me three examples of cancer patients who beat their cancer using his methods. Here are the three true stories he told me:

With severe throat cancer, Jim had only "three months to live"

Dr. Simonton treated his very first patient, Jim M., back in 1971. Jim was 61 at the time. He had advanced throat cancer. By the time he saw Dr. Simonton, a doctor had given him the dreaded news: "You have three months to live."

Dr. Simonton turned Jim's "terminal" cancer completely around by teaching him how to use his imagination to create mental images in three key areas:

1. Healthy images of his body's healing mechanisms
2. Healthy images of the treatment he was receiving
3. Healthy images of cancer as a disease

That third point may seem odd. After all, how can you create a "healthy" image of something as ugly and dangerous as cancer?

As Dr. Simonton told me, most cancer patients have an unhealthy image of the disease. They believe cancer is a powerful and deadly foe that's difficult or impossible to beat. They may visualize cancer as some kind of juggernaut or steamroller that's going to run them over.

This kind of imagery is bad because it can be a self-fulfilling prophecy.

But Dr. Simonton said cancer isn't as strong as most people believe it is. In fact, he pointed out that cancer cells are actually weak, deformed, and confused. No cancer cell has ever been known to attack a healthy cell.

Cancer can't even grow very well inside a strong, healthy body. Cancer can only thrive inside a weakened, unhealthy body. It's that simple.

Within a month, tests showed Jim had no evidence of cancer in his body. Just as surprising, he had no side effects from the high-dose radiation he was receiving. Following this victory, Dr. Simonton went on to heal countless patients using the same counseling method.

Bob, with abdominal cancer, was at the "end stage"

In 1974 Dr. Simonton began working with another "hopeless" cancer patient. Bob G., a 39-year-old man from Houston, Texas, was at the end stage of his cancer. Cancer had spread throughout his abdomen. His doctors offered him no hope because chemotherapy wasn't shrinking his tumors. What's more, the chemo was giving him terrible side effects.

Bob had heard about Dr. Simonton's psychological approach to fighting cancer. It seemed to be his only hope.

Dr. Simonton was in Ft. Worth, Texas, at the time. His phone rang, and Bob told him, "I want to come and see you." Dr. Simonton replied, "I'd be happy to work with you on the phone." Bob responded, "I'll come to your office, and you can decide what to do with me there."

Bob spent three days in Ft. Worth learning Dr. Simonton's methods. In just six weeks he went from extensive disease to no evidence of disease. He has remained free of disease. In fact Bob won the senior racquetball championship for North Carolina in 2005. Not bad for someone who'd been at the "end stage" of a losing battle against cancer in 1974.

Dr. Simonton maintained a close personal friendship with Bob and told me he'd spoken to Bob recently.

Woman whips breast cancer and lung cancer with mind power

A woman who'd had two bouts with breast cancer came to see Dr. Simonton with advanced lung cancer. Using his methods, she was able to go through radiation and chemo with no significant side effects. Dr. Simonton told me she's been free of cancer for five years: "She's thriving."

As you probably know, lung cancer is one of the toughest cancers to beat. The famous TV journalist Peter Jennings couldn't shake his lung cancer — despite being wealthy enough to receive the best care money could buy.

But Dr. Simonton told me, "It's not a matter of

money. You have to tap into your body's healing process." He also admitted this idea isn't new at all. It goes back to Hippocrates, the Father of Medicine, who lived 500 years before Christ.

Surprisingly, Dr. Simonton said our *thoughts* affect our physical health even at the microscopic, sub-cellular level. The key thought for better health is *hope*. Cancer's best friend is the thought and feeling of hopelessness. "Hope is an essential ingredient in living life and regaining health," Dr. Simonton told me.

Dr. Simonton warmly encouraged his long-distance patients to go through his self-help books and CDs, which are still available at the Simonton Cancer Center he founded. The Center also offers retreats for those who believe they could benefit. Patients who want to attend a retreat must first read the two books in the "Patient Package" and start applying the mental imagery techniques.

How to get Dr. Simonton's self-help "Patient Package"

You can get Dr. Simonton's unique "Patient Package" of life-saving information and self-help methods, which includes two books and four CDs. To order this package, you can call the Simonton Cancer Center's office toll free at 800-338-2360. Or you can log onto the clinic's website at www.simontoncenter.com and click on "Bookstore." The cost of the "Patient Package" is $75.

Best of all, there's no downside to Dr. Simonton's methods, and potentially a huge upside. His methods are proven to increase your odds of whipping cancer — even if you opt for standard treatments such as surgery, radiation, and chemo. Plus you can apply his methods even without having to go to the Simonton Cancer Center in person.

As you might expect, there's much resistance in the medical and pharmaceutical establishment to Dr. Simonton's revolutionary and inexpensive life-saving techniques.

Dr. Simonton told me that everyone in the healing profession should honor the mind as a HUGELY important component in health. But if that ever happened, he said, it "would change the power structure, which would change the economics of physicians, hospitals, and the pharmaceutical industry." In short, huge sums of money are at stake in the U.S. cancer treatment industry.

Contact information:

The Simonton Cancer Center
Post Office Box 6607
Malibu, CA 90264
Phone: 800-459-3424; 818-879-7904
Email: simontoncancercenter@msn.com
Website: www.simontoncenter.com

Chapter Twelve

The grandmaster of hyperbaric oxygen therapy

"Hyperbaric oxygen therapy for terminally ill cancer patients is lifesaving," says Dr. David Steenblock, an osteopathic physician and pathologist. "It gives the body a blast of fresh air. It pumps massive amounts of oxygen into the brain. It gives you eight to nine times the oxygen you normally breathe."

It's well established that cancer HATES oxygen. That's why it astounds Dr. Steenblock that most doctors ignore this lifesaving tool. He should know, because he operates four hyperbaric chambers in his clinic in Mission Viejo, California. He can't imagine practicing medicine without them.

Dr. Steenblock gave us a tour of his clinic. Then we enjoyed a fine dinner with him, during which time he gave us his views on the best treatment options for cancer patients today.

He told us, "An advanced cancer patient who's been tortured and radiated and chemotherapized and has lost his appetite is MISERABLE. If you put that patient into a hyperbaric chamber once or twice a day and give him intravenous vitamin C, within a day or two he'll want to start eating again."

Dr. Steenblock explained further, "The hyperbaric oxygen therapy and intravenous vitamin C stimulate the immune system to clean up the debris from the dying tumor. This debris poisons the body and shuts down the immune system and appetite. High doses of natural digestive enzymes would have prevented that by digesting the junk in the body."

Even a cancer patient who looks "hopeless" to other doctors may have hope when Dr. Steenblock uses his natural therapies.

For example, a "terminal" lung cancer patient came to his office, pulling his little cart with his portable oxygen tank. He had an oxygen mask on his face and was huffing and puffing. His face was red, and his capillaries were dilated.

Dr. Steenblock asked him, "What's the problem?"

The man replied, "They say I've got cancer. It's in my lungs. They won't operate because if they take out any more of my lung, I'll die. And if they give me radiation, that'll kill my lung, and that'll kill me. And chemo won't work on it. So I've come to you to see what you can do. They gave me about a month to six weeks to live. Can you help me?"

Dr. Steenblock replied, "I don't know. I'll try."

He put the patient on a Gerson diet (vegetarian), but the man wouldn't follow it. So Dr. Steenblock put him on hyperbaric oxygen therapy plus intravenous Vitamin C at more than 100 grams a day. He also gave him Tagamet (cimetidine), a drug usually prescribed for heartburn and peptic ulcers. Dr. Steenblock says, "I was the first doctor to treat a patient with Tagamet and high dose Vitamin C."

The man didn't die in the predicted month to six weeks. In fact, Dr. Steenblock treated him for about two years. And he did well. He showed up once in a while to get his vitamins.

One day the man called Dr. Steenblock and said, "I've got this terrible pain in my lower abdomen — in my groin." The doctor replied, "Get to the hospital as soon as you can."

The man died on his way to the hospital — not of cancer but of an aneurism. He bled to death internally. And the autopsy showed that his cancer hadn't grown one bit during the last two years of his life.

Professor of pharmacology gets hot under the collar

The effects of intravenous vitamin C never cease to amaze Dr. Steenblock. He once had a conversation with a professor of pharmacology from the University of Chicago who declared, "Vitamin C is dangerous! Anybody who gives vitamin C is crazy and should be put in jail. Vitamin C causes uric acid and kidney stones."

Dr. Steenblock replied calmly, "I disagree. I've given Vitamin C intravenously to 20,000 patients, and I've never seen it cause kidney stones." Instead of listening to and learning from a doctor who knows what he's talking about, this know-it-all professor shut his ears, got hot under the collar, and walked off in a huff.

One day a good-looking 24-year-old college kid walked into Dr. Steenblock's office. He said his father was struggling with pancreatic cancer, and he had some questions. So they started talking, and Dr. Steenblock was explaining the technical aspects of cancer and how the various treatments work.

The young man asked deep, penetrating questions about biochemistry. They were tough questions, but Dr. Steenblock answered them well because he knew the chemistry. Finally he told the young man, "You're not here for your father. You're here for the government, aren't you? Where do you go to school?"

The young man was a student at Berkeley and was working undercover for the state medical authorities. Because of his academic background, he'd gotten keenly interested in their discussion, and he'd allowed his intellectual curiosity to get the better of him.

Dr. Steenblock says he was a smart cookie who knew what he was talking about: "So I offered to hire him because I'm always looking for smart people to work with. They're hard to come by," Dr. Steenblock told us.

Few doctors understand cancer as well as Dr. Steenblock does. That's because he has a great deal of experience as a pathologist, and pathology is a useful background for a doctor who wants to truly know cancer.

Why pathologists know cancer better than other doctors do

Dr. Steenblock explains, "As a pathologist, you do a lot of autopsies. So you get to see how disease affects the body. Everyone's body is different, no matter what.

"When you perform autopsies on cancer victims, you get to know what cancer looks like in the bone. You've sliced the bone and put your fingers in the cancer. You see how it destroys the body, how it goes to the kidneys and into the lung and how it acts in the lung. You get an understanding of how it spreads and how it grows. If you don't see it and feel it, you really don't know it.

"You see the common diseases and the rare ones. You really become familiar with a broad spectrum of diseases. Whenever anyone mentions 'rare' diseases, I've usually seen them at the autopsy table."

Dr. Steenblock's interest in cancer goes back decades. Twenty-five years ago, he and his wife spent the first part of their honeymoon attending the Cancer Control Society's annual convention. He didn't want to miss the opportunity to learn about the most effective cancer treatments for his patients.

Over the years, Dr. Steenblock has amassed one of the largest libraries in the world on holistic and alternative health. He doesn't just collect the books; he reads them. There's almost nothing he doesn't know or hasn't heard of.

Through his vast reading and personal experience, he's found that infections are a major problem in cancer patients. "Cancer patients have deficient immune systems," he explains, "so they often have infections. And you have to get rid of those darn infections. Anti-fungals and anti-bacterials enhance cancer treatment.

"Most doctors still don't believe yeast is a problem, which is incredible! Patients who've seen

15 or 20 doctors without good results have come to me, and I say, 'Aha. Yeast!' They ask me, 'Why didn't any of the other doctors diagnose this?' and I tell them it's because other doctors don't think yeast causes any problems."

Dr. Steenblock's darkfield microscope reveals the culprit: yeast!

For example, Dr. Steenblock told us about an anemia patient suffering from chronic abdominal pain and a bloated stomach. When she came to him she was dying of pain. His darkfield microscope instantly showed she had yeast, so he put her on some anti-fungals. Within a week, all of her pain was gone. With a laugh and a twinkle in his eye, he told us, "Then she went back and told the other doctors what a genius I was."

The other doctors could've seen the yeast. They just weren't looking.

Yeast and fungus are linked to cancer. As Dr. Steenblock says, "The esophagus and the iliocecal valve are the two weakest parts of the body. They're the dirtiest, and they have the most fungus. That's what you find when you do an autopsy of a cancer victim. You also find swelling in that iliocecal area because of back-pressure from the liver." (The iliocecal valve is the valve between the large and small intestines.)

It's important for cancer patients to commit to better nutrition and a healthy lifestyle, says Dr. Steenblock. Otherwise, "You might as well send the patient back to surgery, radiation, and chemo."

But Dr. Steenblock has harsh words for oncologists who scoff at patients who have a rough time going through chemo and radiation. He says these conventional doctors have a poor attitude. They need to bring holistic doctors into their clinics to work together and better serve the patient. He says it's time for the two camps to stop the fighting.

Chemo kills the cancer — and too often kills the patient, too!

As a pathologist, Dr. Steenblock did numerous autopsies on people who were cured of cancer but died from chemotherapy. In pathology work, "You see one body after another with no sign of cancer, but there they are: lying on a cold slab. You start to say, 'Well, wait a second. This chemo and radiation may not always be appropriate.' The younger doctors in particular tend to be too aggressive with the chemo. Using high doses, they kill the cancer — AND the patient!"

Dr. Steenblock says that chronic sinus infections are a hidden cause of cancer and that most doctors don't know how to diagnose them. It's simple, he says. You just tap on the cheekbones or above the eyeball and ask the patient whether it's tender. Then tap between the eyes and ask whether it's tender.

Here are some other signs of hidden sinus infections: (1) If you feel sick and have no reason for suffering from chronic fatigue, (2) if it started when you had a cold six months ago, and (3) if you've been sick and tired ever since then, that's a sign. It's likely that pus is getting into your system and damaging your whole body.

These common infections can kill you

According to Dr. Steenblock, sinus infections can kill you. So can gum disease. Letting these infections run loose in your body is disastrous.

He says the life expectancy in certain parts of the Congo is 29 years; at 29, these people look as if they're 75. They've lost their teeth to gum disease, and they're dying of "old age" at 29. Why? Because they've had chronic infections since childhood. "Infections cause aging like you wouldn't believe, and infection leads to inflammation and aging as well as cancer."

Caffeine kills cancer, if you take it the right way

Surprisingly, one of least expensive and most effective ways to fight cancer is with coffee. "Caffeine is a great killer of cancer; it has a direct effect. This is factual and well established. It's published. You can look it up," says Dr. Steenblock.

But here's the rub: Drinking coffee does cancer patients no good whatsoever. A patient can get the anti-cancer benefits only by taking the coffee rectally, through an enema.

The idea of a coffee enema may sound strange, especially if you're new to the field of alternative cancer treatment. But Dr. Steenblock says it's well established in the medical literature that coffee enemas flush toxins out of the liver and stimulate tumor necrosis factor (TNF), a substance that kills cancer.

For that reason, he believes coffee enemas should be done FIRST, followed by colonic hydrotherapy to clean out the patient's colon.

The patient who called Dr. Steenblock an unprintable name

The day we interviewed Dr. Steenblock, he told us about Nedva, a loyal patient he'd seen earlier in the day. Nedva is now over 90. Back in 1981, when she was in her 60s, she came to Dr. Steenblock with a shoulder problem. He gave her steroids, but the treatment didn't help.

Four months later when she mentioned she was also constipated, Dr. Steenblock told her, "Have a colonic." She replied, "O.K. I'll have one."

A couple of days later, Nedva saw Dr. Steenblock and exclaimed, "What the hell is wrong with you?" He said, "What?" She said, "You *ss hole!" He said, "What? What?"

She asked, "Why didn't you tell me about a colonic? You let me suffer for four months, and after one colonic all my pain is gone. You turkey!" Dr. Steenblock is a gifted storyteller, and we had a good laugh over this story.

Colonic hydrotherapy supports the cancer patient's immune system

Dr. Steenblock said a colonic, surprisingly, often solves joint pain and back pain in a way that makes patients "feel like a million bucks." But getting rid of all the accumulated junk in the colon also helps the immune system, which is crucial for cancer patients.

Dr. Steenblock is deeply interested in cancer, has studied it for decades, and has helped countless patients get rid of cancer and other diseases. But he declares, "I don't treat cancer. I clean up the body. I help bring the infections and inflammation under control. I strengthen the immune system."

The reason Dr. Steenblock doesn't treat cancer is simple: "If you're not doing cut-burn-poison [surgery, radiation, or chemotherapy], you're not practicing 'standard medicine' for cancer treatment. That's where we're at right now in America." Because he doesn't practice medicine the way conventional doctors do, the medical authorities have hassled him.

Dr. Steenblock is hauled before the medical board

For example, the medical board once accused him of using substances that weren't listed in the Physicians' Desk Reference (PDR). He'd prescribed natural substances — zinc, lactobacillus acidophilus, and other nutritional products — to a patient suffering from chronic diarrhea.

The board accused him of medical malpractice, not because he had harmed the patient — he hadn't — but because he wasn't using standard prescription drugs!

Dr. Steenblock won this fight. But it was a nuisance to have to deal with it.

He says, "Where is it written that I must prescribe drugs? Why are medical doctors 'drug doctors'? It's not a law. It's not in writing. The medical boards are brainwashed by the pharmaceutical industry and the medical schools. The medical schools don't teach natural medicine at all. They don't teach anything about vitamins.

"I took a course in pharmacology at the University of California at Irvine Medical School about six years ago. This is the 'drug course' — the course for all the medical students to learn about drugs. Out of that whole course, there was one paragraph about vitamins: two sentences. That's it! They're teaching esoteric, weird stuff that has no bearing whatsoever on the practice of medicine."

Dr. Steenblock has helped many cancer patients and will keep doing so. If he believes another doctor can better serve the patient, he doesn't hesitate to refer the patient to another clinic.

But because of the lack of health freedom in America, Dr. Steenblock doesn't advertise for cancer patients. Nor does he mention cancer on his excellent website. That's because he doesn't want to have a target on his back.

In recent years, Dr. Steenblock's focus has been on helping victims of strokes and brain injuries. His hyperbaric oxygen therapy and other cutting edge therapies enable such patients to achieve astonishing recoveries. What's more, he's found that the same therapies that help cancer patients also do wonders for stroke victims.

For example, he uses an external counter-pulsation device that pushes blood up from the legs during the rest phase of the heart. This stimulates blood vessels to expand and to make new blood vessels, causing increased oxygenation of internal organs.

Remember, cancer hates oxygen. That's how external counter-pulsation gives patients a new lease on life.

Dr. Steenblock has set an ambitious goal: to live to be 120 years old. To reach this goal, he eats right and injects himself with stem cells. He also gives his patients the benefit of stem cell therapy where appropriate. (He doesn't use the controversial embryonic stem cells, which have produced disappointing results. Rather, he uses adult stem cells, with impressive results. He's on the cutting edge of ethical stem cell research.)

Other doctors have invited Dr. Steenblock to join their practices, but he turns these invitations down. He says, "What would I do without my hyperbaric oxygen chambers?" He won't consider practicing medicine without hyperbaric oxygen therapy.

Costs at Dr. Steenblock's clinic vary, depending on each case.

One advantage of going to his clinic is that you get to see Dr. Steenblock himself — one of the great medical pioneers of our time.

Contact information:

David A Steenblock, M.S., D.O.
The Brain Therapeutics Medical Clinic
26381 Crown Valley Parkway, Suite130
Mission Viejo, CA 92691
Toll-free: 800-300-1063
Local: 949-367-8870
Website: www.strokedoctor.com

Chapter Thirteen

The country chiropractor who can even handle leukemia

The first thing you'll notice when you walk into the reception area of Dr. Kent Bartell's Naturopathic medical office is the parrot – a female named Alex. Don't be surprised if Alex starts talking to you.

It makes you laugh, and amusement and laughter have therapeutic value for the cancer patient. Alex and I were starting to develop rapport when the receptionist told me Dr. Bartell was ready for the interview.

Dr. Bartell is one of the rarest of rare birds. He's a naturopath who practices under a chiropractic license, and he can legally administer IVs. He's as smart as a whip and well informed about the most effective natural therapies. He offers an impressive array of these therapies in his clinic. And he can claim some remarkable successes at helping patients beat cancer.

For example, one patient came to him with leukemia that had gone from a chronic state into a full-blown acute blast cell crisis. "You've got less than three months to live," his doctors told him. And they could say it with confidence, because living past three months *never* happens when a leukemia patient enters that crisis.

Dr. Bartell told me, "When this patient came in to see me, his white blood cell count was 300,000 or something – off the charts. He was in really rough shape. We started IV therapies for his immune system. I tell you what. He beat it! His immune system turned it around. He came out of the acute blast cell crisis and reverted into a stage of chronic, stable disease, which he's managing.

"Months later, he went to an oncologist in New York who specializes in leukemias – a renowned leader in his field. He told the doctor about his case, and the fact that he had used natural therapies to come out of the acute blast cell crisis. The doctor replied, 'That's not possible. It never happens. You don't ever come out of it.' He told the doctor, 'You can look at my blood tests.' The doctor replied, 'Well, I'll look at it, but I'm telling you that you didn't. You didn't actually have an *acute* blast cell crisis because it never goes from acute back to chronic.'

"The doctor looked at the records and came back shocked. He said, 'You in fact *did*. I've never seen this in all my years of practice. I don't know what you did, but I want to know everything you did because this is unheard of.' For whatever reason, the doctor must've lost interest because I never heard from him."

Perhaps the doctor changed his mind when he realized that his whole way of practicing medicine might have to change if he discovered the natural therapies that work much better than harsh, conventional treatments.

This success is even more astonishing when you consider that Dr. Bartell isn't an MD. Who would've ever thought that a country chiropractor could accomplish what MDs consider impossible?

Dr. Bartell described another patient who was dealing with Stage Three lymphoma. The patient decided to hedge his bets by doing natural treatments with Dr. Bartell as well as standard chemotherapy, administered by a conventional doctor. The patient had an ugly three-inch tumor that shrank *fast*. But he didn't tell his conventional doctor that he was also receiving natural treatments. He kept that a secret.

The conventional doctor was astounded. He remarked, "This is amazing. We've never seen the chemo shrink the tumor this quickly!" The doctor never did find out the secret. This case is unusual because almost all of Dr. Bartell's patients choose to undergo his natural treatments *instead of* conventional cancer treatments.

Glen was a goner at 84 but lived to be 94

An 84-year-old patient named Glen from Texas had a similar struggle with Stage Three lymphoma, but Glen had tumors just about everywhere. His situation was serious. He could only do one week of treatments at Dr. Bartell's clinic, which cost about $3,000.

During that week, Dr. Bartell pulled out all the stops to jumpstart Glen's deteriorated health. "We did everything," said Dr. Bartell. And when Glen left at the end of the week, Dr. Bartell gave him a health plan he could follow at home.

Dr. Bartell told me, "While he was working the program at home in Texas, he got pneumonia, but he pulled out of it. He beat the pneumonia, and his doctors were shocked because they were certain the pneumonia would take him out. He had a great attitude and commitment and got a clean bill of health after eight months. He lived for another 10 years and died of something other than cancer at the age of 94."

That last story is significant for a couple of reasons. (1) Dr. Bartell's clinic is among the least expensive alternative cancer clinics I've ever visited. (2) Although Dr. Bartell prefers to have patients stay for more than one week of treatment, he's willing to work within their time and money constraints. If a patient can only afford to stay at the clinic for a week, Dr. Bartell will do his best to initiate a turnaround in the patient's health during that week and to point him in the right direction when the patient leaves at the end of the week.

The reality is this: No matter how long a patient stays at the clinic, the patient must go home sometime. And at home it's essential for the patient to follow a health plan to keep the cancer from sneaking back. How long is it necessary to follow this health plan at home? For as long as the patient wants to live!

Here's what Dr. Bartell told me as he gave me a tour of his clinic:

"I deal with a lot of cancer patients, so I focus on the immune system. Therefore, it's necessary to look at the nervous system. Stress can weaken the immune system. Here's a therapy [pointing to a device] that helps a patient relax: a sound frequency therapy that uses music. It takes about an hour. The patient uses it with infrared to get infrared benefit. It's sound and vibration. The music, which is all instrumental, helps to synchronize the body and bring the brain waves down from the stress mode.

"I also have a Tesla unit that has a smorgasbord of frequencies that help bring balance to the body. It also raises the voltage of the body, raising the 'charge' of the nervous system. It helps the body. Sometimes people sleep when they have this therapy.

"This is our colonic hydrotherapy room. Detox is important. We eliminate many toxins through the colon.

Patients can feel the circulation benefits all over

"Here's the Chi machine [a device about the size of a bread box] for lymphatic movement. Patients lie down and put their ankles on the device. When you turn on the device, it creates a wave-like motion. When it's over, the patient can feel the circulation benefits all over. Many patients buy a machine so they can use it at home twice a day. A Chi machine costs about $250.

"What I do here with patients is not 'the program.' Rather, it's a jumpstart to the program. The program is what they do when they go home, which I outline for each patient. Patients come in here because they need a big boost to jumpstart their healing. It takes time to heal, to detox, to build the immune system. It can take weeks or longer for the body to get its strength and health back. The body must become strong long-term.

"If the body has been going downhill for seven years, it takes about a year to turn that around. You have to race for time with cancer. My ideal would be not to have a clinic at all but for patients to do the right things at home.

"This is my IV room. We do IV therapies here: oxidative IVs, high potency vitamin C, chelation IVs. High potency nutrition through IV boosts the immune system and builds the body up.

"We have a massage therapist who gives patients a relaxing and gentle lymphatic massage.

"Here's our hyperbaric oxygen chamber, which holds one person. [It's a metal chamber, not a vinyl tent, so it can withstand double the pressure of the inflatable models. This is impressive!] Hyperbaric oxygen therapy takes an hour.

Some patients convert a small closet into a home sauna

"I'm a big proponent of sauna therapy because it increases blood circulation."

Dr. Bartell added near-infrared lamps to his far-infrared to give the patient the maximum benefit. He also gives his patients information on how they can build an effective but inexpensive infrared sauna at home if they can't afford an expensive ready-made model.

The patient can even convert a small closet into an infrared sauna: in that case, the patient only needs to add infrared lamps and a stool or chair.

"For my patients," he continued, "I feel infrared saunas offer great benefits for detox, for circulation, and for the nervous system because there's a calming effect. It should be done at home twice a day, morning and evening. It's an at-home therapy I typically recommend. I also recommend Dr. Larry Wilson's book *Sauna Therapy for Detoxification and Healing*.

"I do precision far infrared therapy, which is local hyperthermia. [Hyperthermia is a therapy in which cancer cells are killed by heating them to fever-like temperatures. It's popular and highly regarded among experts on alternative cancer treatment.] It gets hot. Dr. Kazuko brought this device to the U.S., and she spoke at the Cancer Control Convention a few years ago. That's where I found out about it. I did some training with Dr. Kazuko, and I like that therapy. You can apply heat several inches deep to a trouble spot and create some changes with that.

"Here's our UVBI machine for ultraviolet blood irradiation. One of the effects is that it actually produces oxygen in the blood. I encourage patients to get ozone generators for their home."

In ultraviolet blood irradiation, a small amount of blood is withdrawn from the patient and exposed to ultraviolet light. Then the irradiated blood is returned to the patient's body.

This simple, nontoxic, harmless treatment produces astounding results not only for cancer but for a wide variety of medical conditions including infections. It was on its way to becoming an accepted treatment for polio before the polio vaccine was developed. Tragically, mainstream medicine has forgotten this exciting therapy, but it's being used to great effect by many alternative and integrative doctors.

Thermography beats mammograms hands down!

Continuing on our tour, Dr. Bartell pointed to another device. "Here's where we do infrared thermography, which looks for hot spots on the surface of the skin, which can indicate a problem area below the surface. With thermography you can actually find a developing cancer area *six years earlier* than with mammograms! Each time a woman has a mammogram, she increases her risk of breast cancer by one percent. There's more valid research behind infrared thermography than for mammography. Thermography isn't diagnostic in the strict sense, but it can indicate a red flag that needs further investigation.

"We test the patient's hair for heavy metals. When you look at a 1.5-inch length of hair, you're looking at a three month history. Analytical Research Lab does this test. Testing the patient's hair demonstrates the detoxifying benefits of sauna therapy because 1.5 inches of hair shows changes in heavy metal levels over time.

"Blood tests are crucial. Most doctors don't look at the percentage and ratios of the white blood cells. That ratio can give you a perspective on the strength of the immune system. A complete blood count with differential shows about ten things including ratios. Of the five types of white blood cells, almost all of them are either neutrophils, which are usually about 65 percent of the total, or lymphocytes, usually about 35 percent. Neutrophils go after bacteria. Lymphocytes go after viruses. The percentage between the two is significant.

What to look for when you get a comprehensive blood test

"Lymphocytes should be at about 35 percent. Rarely do I see someone who has cancer who's around 35 percent. It'll usually be in the teens, or if the patient has leukemia it'll be above 40 percent. It's out of balance. You want the absolute number of lymphocytes to come in between 1.8 and 2.0. The perfect mark is 1.9.

"I approach cancer like a chronic infection the body has been dealing with and fighting. Most people say they haven't been sick, and they're shocked that they have cancer. Their body has been ignoring things on an acute level and letting things fester.

"The immune system needs to deal with things on a chronic level, and all cancer is a chronic condition. It can be caused by physical trauma. For example, a woman who's been hit or elbowed in the breast could develop cancer where she was bruised. The radiation from a mammogram is another kind of trauma that can cause cancer. Conventional doctors recommend that women have a mammogram once a year. Thirty mammograms gives a woman a 30 percent risk of breast cancer. Cancer will develop in the most vulnerable spot in the body.

The right way to juice

"As for diet, I recommend a low-sugar plan with live foods in which the enzymes are active. Juicing is beneficial. Juicing gives you nutrients during a juice fast. No more than 15 percent of the juice should be fruit juice.

"When you're juicing, you can mix fruits and vegetables – apples and carrots, for example. I've had lung cancer patients who've done juice fasts for several months, drinking a gallon of juice a day to keep up their energy. They bring their juice to work. I'm talking about juicing [as opposed to blenders like Vitamix and Blendtec that create a vegetable slush]. The patient should throw away the pulp, which has most of the toxins. When patients juice, they have extra energy available because no energy is required to digest juice.

"Leafy vegetables are great. The patient should stay away from high-starch food. I'm not a proponent of dairy, but natural yogurt and raw goat milk are fine. Dairy causes mucus to form. And after we're two years old, our bodies no longer have the lactase enzyme needed to digest milk. But natural raw goat milk is fine. I don't advocate a lot of heavy meats, and I recommend no pork. I advocate a Kosher approach.

"I do little chiropractic, though I'll do it when necessary. My focus is on holistic alternative medicine. My card says Naturopathic D.C. I practice as a Naturopathic doctor underneath the chiropractic license.

"I'm kind of like a coach. The word 'doctor' comes from doctrine, which means teaching. Doctors have moved away from being doctors toward being physicians who give drugs and do surgeries. They rarely get at the root of the problem. They don't practice health care but disease care: if you don't have a disease, they don't care, and they tell you to come back when you finally have a disease. But imbalances come well before someone is diagnosed with a disease.

"I ask, 'Where are the imbalances?' By the time some people actually come down with a disease, it can be difficult or impossible to reverse it.

"My patients come to me desperate. When we do

things that promote health, we often see the patient live two or three times longer than a conventional doctor predicted. Sometimes we can beat the condition altogether. I never want to give false hope.

"I never make a claim of curing any disease. I don't cure disease. I help the body get stronger. If the body heals itself, that's the body, not me. I try to figure out where the body is out of balance and help bring it back into balance. My patients trust me. My advertising is by word of mouth. I keep low key. And I've built a national reputation.

"My patients come from all over the country, and most of them can't stay for more than a week or two. It typically it costs about $3,000 per week when they're doing the full program. My clinic is less expensive than most other clinics [It certainly is!]. Patients are in the clinic doing therapies from nine to five, Monday through Friday. Sometimes they get out a little early – at two or three in the afternoon."

The clinic's website offers patients several options for lodging. This is the ideal clinic for cancer patients on a tight budget who want to take responsibility for their health. But even some wealthy patients will choose this clinic because of the extraordinary therapies Dr. Bartell offers.

Contact information:

Dr. Kent Bartell, D.C.
New Hope Health Clinic
121 S 2nd St
Jenks, OK 74037
Phone: 918-298-8810
Website:
www.newhopehealthclinic.com

Chapter Fourteen

The doctor who believes you can cure your cancer at home

When I arrived at Dr. Carlos Garcia's Utopia Wellness clinic for my appointment, the receptionist, Roxana, greeted me and gave me a tour of the clinic. It so happened that the clinic was having an open house holiday party during my visit on December 14th, and everyone was in a celebratory mood.

Roxana walked me through the clinic, showing me the hyperbaric oxygen chamber, the room for colonic hydrotherapy, and the IV room. Dr. Garcia administers a number of different healing substances by IV, including cesium (a natural, non-toxic mineral that goes right to the cancer cells and puts them in an alkaline state that damages or kills them), selenium, vitamin C, and the B vitamins.

The patients were all upbeat and optimistic. I detected no defeatism or negativity in any of their faces. Roxana told me that patients come to Dr. Garcia's clinic from all 50 states and even from foreign countries in South America and Africa.

Dr. Carlos Garcia, M.D., is an unusual doctor for many reasons. Because he advocates natural and traditional ways of healing instead of harsh drugs with ghastly side effects, a band of Native Americans has adopted him as their "medicine man."

What's even more remarkable is that my friend and fellow health freedom advocate Bill Henderson asked Dr. Garcia to co-author the fourth edition of his popular book *Cancer-Free: Your Guide to Gentle, Non-toxic Healing*. Bill is an enthusiast for home cancer cures, although he's not opposed to cancer patients' seeking help from alternative cancer doctors.

You might wonder why Dr. Garcia, who runs a cancer clinic, advocates and promotes certain home cures for cancer. The answer is simple: No matter how good a clinic may be, the patients have to go home sometime. And what the patients do at home is crucial for keeping the cancer from sneaking back.

So even cancer patients who go to a clinic for cancer treatment need a home "cure" – that is, a health plan to keep cancer away for the rest of their lives.

To prevent cancer from coming back, Dr. Garcia and Bill Henderson say the patient needs seven things:

1. The cancer patient's sagging immune system needs help. Dr. Garcia recommends the Transfer Point brand of beta glucan to boost the immune system.
2. To improve the oxygenation of the cancer patient's cells, Dr. Garcia likes the Budwig protocol, a mixture of flax seed oil and cottage cheese that is one of the most widely-used home cancer treatments.
3. To help stop cancer from spreading, Dr. Garcia recommends that patients take a nutritional supplement with vitamin C and L-lysine/L-proline with green tea extract.
4. Greens and enzymes help make the patient's body alkaline and provide the enzymes the patient needs. According to leading authorities on alternative cancer treatment, when the body is acidic it is

vulnerable to disease. Proper nutrition and supplementation keep the body alkaline and highly resistant to disease.

5. A cancer-fighting eating plan helps detoxify the patient's body and restore its balance. The most effective eating plan avoids sugar, processed food, animal protein, dairy (except for the cottage cheese that's mixed with flax oil in the Budwig protocol), and gluten.
6. A vitamin-mineral supplement is recommended that covers all the needed essentials.
7. Additional Vitamin D3 gives an extra boost to the nutrients above.

For more details about this home cure, you can get the best-selling book Dr. Garcia wrote with Bill Henderson, *Cancer-Free: Your Guide to Gentle, Non-toxic Healing*, on this website: http://naturalcancerremedies.com/fourthedition/index.html. The popular Special Report *How to Cure Almost Any Cancer at Home for $5.15 a Day* by Bill Henderson with Andrew Scholberg is available at www.CureCancerAtHome.com/515/. (The Special Report is a condensed version of the recommendations found in *Cancer-Free*.)

While the home cure is a good long-term strategy for health, many cancer patients go to an alternative clinic to "jumpstart" their health turnaround, and that's what Dr. Garcia offers at his clinic.

Dr. Garcia's six-pronged holistic approach to cancer

Dr. Garcia doesn't just treat symptoms. His six-pronged holistic approach deals with the root causes of cancer.

Prong One: Fortify. Dr. Garcia says, "One way we fortify the patient is a specialized combination of nutrients and natural substances used as a targeted cancer therapy depending on the individual needs of the patient. The other way, which also depends on the needs of the patient, is a more general approach seeking to boost strength and the immune system. Utopia Wellness offers these treatments intravenously, because you cannot get adequate levels to destroy cancer cells by taking them orally."

Prong Two: Clarify. As Dr. Garcia explains, "Mind-body medicine is an increasingly important part of cancer treatment. Mind-body medicine explores the influence of your mind, emotions, and traumas on your body, immune system, and vice versa. Some studies have suggested that addressing your psychological and spiritual health (including mood, attitudes, self-image, and outlook) can help promote recovery from cancer.

"The mind-body medicine team at Utopia consists of experienced, compassionate facilitators," Dr. Garcia told me. "The goal is to help you deal with the physical and emotional issues that may be interfering with your recovery."

Prong Three: Detoxify. "The air we breathe, the water we drink, and the food we eat are filled with man-made chemicals and pesticides that overload the liver and the entire immune system. Internally, your body is continually at work to keep itself clean," Dr. Garcia told me in our interview. "Your skin, liver, lungs, kidneys, lymphatic system, and colon perform together to keep these toxins and wastes moving through naturally. When you have cancer, your detoxification system must work even harder and can benefit from a complete detoxification program.

"Colon Therapy is an integral part of Utopia's detoxification program. The goal is to remove waste and toxins that have built up over time, allowing your digestive system to function more efficiently. Your immune system is strengthened because toxins are washed away before they have a chance to harm your health, and your body will absorb more nutrients from food."

Utopia Wellness also gives its patients herbs and nutritional supplements to help the organs detoxify. For lymphatic drainage, which is essential to detoxification, the clinic provides lymphatic massage.

Prong Four: Modify. Dr. Garcia gives this advice to cancer patients: "If you have cancer, what you DON'T eat is as important as what you DO eat. The key to our nutritional program is the Budwig diet. One of the most important and far reaching health discoveries of the 20th century is that made by Dr. Johanna Budwig, a German biochemist who became a leading European authority on fats and nutrition. She was nominated for the Nobel Prize seven times. She used her methods to successfully heal terminal cancer patients, as well as people with heart diseases, arthritis and other ailments."

Prong Five: Alkalinize. Dr. Garcia says, "Cancer thrives in an acidic environment so part of the program at Utopia includes alkalinizing the body. In addition to the Budwig components of the nutritional program for cancer patients, Utopia recommends a diet consisting of organic whole foods that cause the body to become more alkaline. Unfortunately, all too often a person's pH tends to be too acidic, making a good alkaline cancer treatment even more important. Utopia believes that an alkaline pH protects the body against cancer, and can even help to cure it once it has developed. Consuming certain fresh organically grown vegetables and drinking alkaline water will help you achieve alkalinity."

One of the most effective minerals for making the body alkaline is cesium, which Dr. Garcia administers to cancer patients by IV.

Prong Six: Oxygenize. Because cancer cells hate oxygen, Dr. Garcia gives his cancer patients an oxygen boost with chelation therapy and hyperbaric oxygen therapy.

"Chelation therapy is thought to improve circulation throughout the body, reduce misplaced soft-tissue calcification, and increase oxygen to cells by binding to toxic heavy metals," he explained to me. "Hyperbaric oxygen therapy delivers 100% pure oxygen to you through increased atmospheric pressure in an enclosed chamber. When oxygen (O_2) is delivered at higher than normal pressure, your body is able to absorb more of it into your blood cells, blood plasma, cerebral-spinal fluid, and other bodily fluids. Once in the chamber, your body responds by reducing inflammation, which results in increased blood flow to oxygen-deprived areas. The air that we breathe normally contains 21 percent oxygen. Breathing in 100 percent oxygen under increased pressure within a hyperbaric chamber allows extra oxygen to be forced into the blood stream and dissolved at a much faster rate than if pressure is not used."

Stage Four colon cancer patient hits rock bottom before discovering Utopia

One colon cancer patient, Nancy W., was going through unimaginable misery until she discovered Utopia Wellness. Here's Nancy's story in her own words:

"In March of 2007 I was diagnosed with Colon Cancer. I had 10 out of 12 chemotherapy treatments. I had to stop the chemo because my head would swell so bad I felt like I was choking all the time. Also if I dropped anything, I would almost pass out when I bent to pick it up. I spent at least 3 days on the sofa in a deep sleep. The rest of the time I would be so tired I could hardly walk. I also lost my hair. My previous doctors said that diet has nothing to do with cancer; it was 'okay' to eat my steak and potatoes and drink a glass of wine. Now I know this not to be true. Finding the right doctor has educated me.

"Dr. Garcia says that diet and a good frame of mind is important to our healing. After my 10th chemo treatment I told my doctor I had an achy feeling in my right ovary. He ordered an ultrasound and found a mass. The doctors went in and removed it. Before the ovary was taken out, a pelvic washing was done and micro cells of cancer were found in my pelvic area, meaning my cancer was in Stage Four. We then looked for a surgeon to do the procedure called debulking. This procedure puts you on the operating table for about eight hours with a four-day hospital stay. With this surgery they also pour a very hot chemo inside your pelvic area. They let it set for two hours, then they clean and sew you back together. This operation has caused me the most problems, and I am still sore inside. I have lost a lot of weight and it has been close to nine months.

"I wish I would have found Dr. Garcia and his team when I was first diagnosed. I would never have had the surgeries or the chemo unless it was suggested by the doctor. I have had six weeks of Dr. Garcia's cancer protocol and thru testing with a PET scan and blood work, no cancer has been found.

"This is the place to come. The entire staff, including the front office, accounting, and the nurses, are friendly, warm and knowledgeable. The doctor's door is always open to you if you have any questions.

"The most important thing to me is the quality of my life. My head is clear. I have energy and I'm back to the old Nancy, and in the process I am killing cancer cells. Now tell me, can it get any better than that? Here at Utopia in Clearwater, Florida we are like one big family. We share our stories and we laugh a lot."

Stage Four breast cancer patient gets new lease on life

Seventy-three-year-old Mary Z. is another patient who discovered the Utopia Wellness clinic when she was at the edge of the grave with Stage Four breast cancer. This is her story in her own words:

"My son was talking to a friend of his who had Stage Four prostate cancer, and lo and behold, he was told by the oncologist at the Veterans Affairs office where he was going, that he had about six months to live, and they couldn't do anything for him but make him comfortable. Well, it turns out somehow he found out about the Utopia Wellness clinic and after only eight weeks of treatment, he was miraculously cancer free! When my son told me this, I was rather skeptical, but my son was relentless and pushed me to go. We went together about two and a half months ago.

"When I first met Dr. Garcia, I was a bit taken aback by his methods. Instead of just talking about tests, and cutting, and radiation, and chemo, he talked about things like my diet, my thought process, what was going on in my life emotionally, spiritually. I remember telling my son on the way home that I really wasn't too sure about this. But after much thought, I decided what did I really have to lose? I went for it. Boy was that a great decision!

"Dr. Garcia put me on a rigorous cancer protocol which included intravenous vitamins, colonic hydrotherapy, lymphatic massage, hyperbaric oxygen, ionic foot baths, talk therapy, and spiritual counseling. Most importantly, in my opinion, Dr. Garcia focused not only on removing unhealthy foods and eating habits out of my life, but removing big stresses. He did it in such a way that showed immense care and love for me. He was a bit stern at times, but I really don't know if I could have made it through such a program without it!

"So fast forward eight weeks, I went to have a follow-up PET scan done, and where the lung spots were, there was nothing. Where the lymphs were infected, there was nothing. My liver looked clear, and not only did Dr. Garcia tell me, 'You're cancer free,' so did my oncologist! The oncologist was amazed that it had cleared up!

"What a relief it was, and what a great feeling of not only knowing that in such a short time what I thought was a death sentence was eradicated, but that I really had my hand in getting better! If it were not for my adhering to a strict diet, really changing the way I think and the way I handle stresses in life, and the way I generally carry myself, things may have ended up differently.

"Not only does Dr. Garcia give you the care you need, the treatments you need, the talks you need, the guidance you need, he most importantly gives you the tools you need to get *rid* of the cancer, and know for a surety that it won't come back! What a great feeling!

"I highly recommend Utopia Wellness clinic! Not only is Doctor Garcia a breath of fresh air, but also his staff members are well trained, and work together hand in hand to make each patient feel comfortable, feel confident, and feel loved. I am proud to say I am cancer free!"

Utopia clinic is an outpatient facility. Patients from out of town may stay at one of the nearby hotels the clinic recommends. The cost of treatment depends on what's needed for each individual patient and how long the patient stays.

Contact information:

Dr. Carlos Garcia, M.D.
Utopia Wellness
110 State Street Oldsmar, FL 34677
Phone: 727-799-9060
Website: www.UtopiaAwaits.com

Chapter Fifteen

The "hands on" doctor who gets to the root cause of cancer

Dr. Charlie Schwengel, DO, MD(H), is a rare bird. Not only is he an osteopathic physician but he's also a homeopath. When I met him at his clinic, Shea Medical, in Scottsdale, AZ, he greeted me in a folksy way with a warm smile. I complimented him on his silver bolo tie, a symbol of the Southwest which Dr. Schwengel wears with pride.

In addition to such therapies as vitamin C by IV, ozone, peroxide, chelation, and Insulin Potentiation Therapy (IPT), Dr. Schwengel uses German New Medicine, a healing strategy developed by Dr. Ryke Geerd Hamer. According to Dr. Hamer, cancer develops following an emotional trauma such as the loss of a job, a divorce, or the death of a loved one, to name just a few typical examples.

An emotional trauma causes stress. Stress can be good when it prompts us to react to something like screeching brakes or an attack by a bear. But unrelenting stress – distress – can tear down the immune system and set the stage for cancer. When it is chronic or long term, stress is a killer.

Dr. Schwengel is convinced that Dr. Hamer is right. He told me, "In virtually every case of cancer, I find it's the result of an emotional trauma. Why cancer appears is as unique as each person's story. I look for that in every patient and help the patients relieve the distress so they can heal. I know how to open up the door to the patient's emotional trauma. That's what you have to do to heal it.

"One patient might be in anguish because he couldn't protect his daughter. Another might feel worthless. Another might be angry with something or somebody. To heal the cancer, these problems must be faced and dealt with."

For example, one of Dr. Schwengel's patients felt unforgiving anger toward his daughter, who was in prison for selling illegal drugs. Because his dominant emotion was unrelenting anger, it's in keeping with German New Medicine theory that he came down with liver cancer.

Dr. Schwengel told me, "He healed his relationship with his daughter. THAT is healing! Healing at the emotional level is there. We see that with just about every patient we treat. I tell cancer patients, 'Don't be afraid to open the closet, let in some light, and let the "ghosts" out.'"

According to Dr. Schwengel, *everything* is important: vitamins, minerals, nutrition, detoxifying, sometimes a little bit of chemotherapy (low dose chemo with IPT). In his view, "Cancer patients typically get locked into the idea of having to 'fight' cancer. When they get diagnosed with cancer, they feel they have to start fighting. But there's nothing healing about fighting.

"Fighting always triggers and encourages more cancer growth because of the stress. You don't heal and fight at the same time. You have to remove the stress to heal. Here at our clinic we help patients let go of the idea of fighting and shift their focus to healing. Patients who do that will do just fine."

How his mother cured herself when doctors gave her only three months to live

Dr. Schwengel said, "My mother is a good example of that. When her doctors told her she had three months to live because of her Stage Four melanoma and lymphoma, they said she had to start chemo right away! She went to a health food store instead. That was 30 years ago – she's an example of a CURE from Stage Four! It can be done. It's a matter of mindset."

I asked Dr. Schwengel to tell me his story. He said he wanted to be a chiropractor at first. He liked the idea of a hands-on approach that relieved patients' pain. Then someone suggested osteopathy, and that appealed to him even more. He liked the medical education offered in osteopathic school plus the hands-on application.

Other treatments Dr. Schwengel likes to use are prolotherapy and prolozone, which involve natural injections. He told me, "Joints are held together by ligaments. When ligaments become loose, they sag. The sagging creates pain. We do injections into the ligaments to stimulate them to heal. That's what prolotherapy is about. Not a lot of doctors know how to do it."

How his dad turned from grey and ashen to pink, hale, and hearty

Dr. Schwengel learned about homeopathic medicine when he was in school. His dad was at death's door. His pallor was grey and ashen. But when an alternative doctor gave him some chelation treatments, he turned pink, hale, and hearty. Chelation therapy removes toxins from the body. Those treatments turned his dad's life around.

Dr. Schwengel's philosophy is to do what works, which is why he believes so strongly in nutrition and energy therapy. He says, "You can't be healthy on drugs."

The fact that Dr. Schwengel is licensed as a homeopathic doctor, in addition to holding an osteopathic medical license, gives him a layer of protection from harassment by conventional medical authorities. These authorities may not approve of some of his "alternative" treatments, but those treatments are authorized by the homeopathic medical board.

Dr. Schwengel told me, "People like to ask me, 'What's your success rate?' But the success rate belongs to the patient, not the doctor. We can't impose health on people. We can't force them to be well. We *could* use forceful therapies like chemo and radiation. But healing comes from the inside. People do great here at the clinic. But if they slip back into old habits that caused the cancer, it comes back. When people take responsibility, the way my mother did, they see good results.

"The conventional cancer treatments – chemo and radiation – are so bad that most cancer patients would be better off refusing all treatment than to go the conventional route. But they need help. And that's where this clinic shines.

"Conventional doctors want to start chemo the day after cancer is diagnosed, but the first treatment that's necessary is a couple of weeks of cleansing. Cleansing gets rid of the biofilms located around the tumors or germs you want to treat. Our strategy is to do two weeks of cleansing, followed by low-dose chemotherapy with IPT while we build up the immune system. By following that approach we get much better results."

Legendary doctor's counseling method can cure cancer!

Dr. Schwengel's wife works at the clinic as a massage therapist. She's a lymphatic drainage specialist, which requires the lightest touch in massage. She's also skilled at balancing the patient's body so that energy – known as qi in Chinese medicine – flows freely.

In addition, I was impressed to discover that she has learned the counseling techniques of the late Dr. O. Carl Simonton and that she does counseling with patients once a week. (We discussed Dr. Simonton's approach in Chapter 11.)

For her own lymphatic drainage, Dr. Schwengel's wife uses a mini-trampoline every day. I asked her, "What kind do you recommend?"

She said, "I like the original ReboundAIR. I bought one in the late 1970s, and it lasted 30 years. I bought a new one that has a lifetime warranty. It folds in half, and the legs fold in so it can be stored more easily. It cost about $180."

She told me it's not necessary to bounce high, and she recommended landing on the heels to move more lymph. I asked her how long she recommends bouncing. She said not more than 20 minutes, but five minutes is better than nothing.

Pancreatic cancer patient finds hope and healing

Arizona resident Leonard Brogdon, a senior citizen, thought his pancreatic cancer diagnosis was a death sentence. After he discovered Dr. Schwengel's clinic, he was happy to discover he was wrong. Here is his story as told by his wife:

"When my husband was diagnosed with inoperable pancreatic cancer in March of 2013 at the age of 67, our lives were forever changed. We were devastated when the doctor at first told us that the tumor was operable, only to find out later that it was not.

"My daughter began to research the clinics in Arizona, as that is our home state. Prior to our finding Shea Medical, we had been bombarded with numerous alternatives. The traditional medical community offered large doses of chemotherapy with only a 20 percent chance of reducing the tumor size, which was a grim prognosis for extending the quality and length of his life.

"We believe that we were divinely led to Shea Medical and Dr. Charlie Schwengel. My daughter spoke to the Patient Care Coordinator, Dana Van Hoose, and a meeting was set up for us to see the clinic, meet the doctor and the staff. That meeting changed our lives, turning our desperation to hope. Finally, after being overwhelmed with so many 'cancer cures' that are out there, we immediately felt the peace that we were in the right place.

"Lenny began an eight-week program using the protocol that was recommended for his type of cancer. From the beginning of our journey with Shea Medical, we felt loved, cared for and comfortable in the atmosphere. Unlike a hospital setting or a doctor's office, this clinic was warm and inviting, and the staff was wonderful in making us feel like we were their only patients. The quality of the care, the expertise and knowledge that they have is truly amazing. Finally, we were given hope and a roadmap to recovery.

"Lenny's tumor marker was reduced by more than half in a few short weeks, and is continuing to decrease at a phenomenal rate with the treatment that Shea Medical provides. He is feeling much better now. We can't say enough praise to describe our experience with Shea Medical and every one of the staff members. We know that God answered our prayers and all the prayers across the country in leading us to them."

Four out of five patients who come to Dr. Schwengel for treatment fly into Phoenix or drive from out of state. Patients stay at one of several resorts with which the clinics have a partnership. Patients on a tight budget stay at the Zona Hotel and Suites, which is set up for extended stays. Each suite has a kitchen. This hotel's average cost for patients staying four weeks or more is less than $30 a night – more than reasonable.

Contact information:

Dr. Charlie Schwengel, D.O., MD(H)
Shea Medical
12002 E Shea Blvd, Suite 5
Scottsdale, AZ 85259
Phone: 480-657-7000
Website: www.SheaMedical.com

Chapter Sixteen

The cancer victim who fired her doctors, healed herself, and became a holistic doctor to heal others

"In 21 days you can just about get rid of any cancer," said Dr. Renee Welhouse, N.D., Ph.D.

In 1971, Renee Welhouse, a Midwestern woman from Wisconsin, was just in her 20s when she got the heartbreaking news: She had cancer — the big "C." Her doctors said drastic surgery was necessary. They rushed her onto an operating table for a bilateral mastectomy.

But that was only the start of her cancer nightmare. The cancer kept coming back, appearing in various organs of her body.

So between 1971 and 1985 Renee underwent 15 surgeries including a hysterectomy, a thyroidectomy, and an unsuccessful bone marrow transplant.

In 1985 her doctors told her she needed two more drastic surgeries to save her life: a leg amputation and a liver transplant. By then Renee was weary of all the surgeries, radiation treatments, chemotherapies, and drugs.

A "miracle" in Bible class

Because her illness was grave, Renee turned to her faith and prepared to meet her Maker. Then a woman in her Bible study class said she knew a lot about natural healing methods. The woman told Renee, "Oh, you can get over this. You just don't poop right, and you have parasites."

Renee thought the woman was nuts! It sounded like the most ridiculous thing she'd ever heard.

Then the woman handed her a book, *Tissue Cleansing through Bowel Management,* by Dr. Bernard Jensen, N.D., D.C. When she read the title, Renee rolled her eyes and thought, "Give me a break!" After all, her doctors said she needed a leg amputation and a liver transplant. How could this woman know more than the doctors?

Renee told me, "When you don't have long to live, you do some pretty unusual things. My husband rented a villa on Jamaica Beach in Texas for a month. We went down there, and after about two weeks I finally read that book because I didn't have anything else to read. And it changed my life.

"At the time, I had an arsenal of industrial-strength prescription drugs in the bathroom: Prednisone, steroids, oral chemo — all kinds of stuff. And I flushed them all down the toilet! My liver enzymes were shot because of all the Prednisone, and my liver went crazy. It was just one thing after another. And so I just threw all those drugs away and never went back. That was 22 years ago."

How Renee healed herself after firing her doctors

When I interviewed Renee, she was still completely free of cancer. She still had both legs, and her original liver was in tiptop shape. She was the picture of health. She regained her health by *disobeying* and *firing* all of her doctors.

She concluded that her doctors were *just plain wrong*. And time proved her right.

How did Renee heal herself ? She cleaned out her colon and got her guts working right. She got rid of her parasites. She detoxified her whole body. And she started eating right — with special attention to proper food-combining principles. In short, she followed to the letter the advice of Dr. Bernard Jensen, the author of the book she'd read at Jamaica Beach.

Having whipped her "hopeless" and "terminal" case of cancer, Renee was astounded by the natural healing power of the human body. To say that Dr. Jensen's book gave her a new lease on life would be an understatement. So she sought out the man whose book had saved her life and studied directly under him, learning all of Dr. Jensen's health secrets.

Dr. Renee thought long and hard about what might have caused her cancer. She strongly suspected the culprit was the polio vaccine she had received as a child.

Cancer: look beyond the symptom to the cause

Eventually Renee became a naturopathic doctor herself and entered private practice to share her remarkable health secrets with cancer victims and people suffering from other health problems. Along the way she also earned a Ph.D. in nutrition.

In 1996 Dr. Renee also interned at American Biologics to master the Bradford BVPM® High Resolution Microscopy System for peripheral blood assessments. Admittedly, that's a mouthful, but it's easy to remember as the darkfield microscope mentioned in previous chapters and used by a number of alternative and integrative doctors.

A darkfield microscope is far superior to the typical microscope a doctor might have in his office. This incredibly powerful scientific instrument, which costs about $20,000, magnifies the patient's blood 14,000 times. It also displays the magnified image on a large video monitor for both the patient and the doctor to see.

Only about 200 to 400 such microscopes are in use in American clinics, according to the best information we have.

Dr. Renee called her darkfield microscope "indispensable" in her practice. This powerful tool, along with analysis of the patient's saliva and urine, gives a razor-sharp picture of the patient's health.

It's puzzling that so few doctors in America are using the darkfield microscope, which would show them at a glance a great deal of valuable information about their patients' health - and also makes it easy to show the patient the same information on the big screen and explain why changes are needed.

Dr. Renee told me, "Cancer is just a symptom of a deeper underlying problem. When you identify and solve this problem, the cancer disappears." She added, "In 21 days you can just about get rid of any cancer." And she proved it over and over — one patient at a time.

She helped so many people get rid of cancer that the government took notice of her.

Government officials burst into Dr. Renee's office to seize her $20,000 microscope

One day in 1999, government agents burst into Dr. Renee's office and told her they were going to confiscate her darkfield microscope. They said it was illegal for her to use it.

Dr. Renee fought them. She told them she had a Ph.D. in nutrition and needed the microscope for her research. She also told them she was a member of the research board of the Bradford Institute in Chula Vista, California. She explained that her research for the Bradford Institute required a darkfield microscope.

Microscope shows what the government doesn't want you to see

The government agents grudgingly backed off from their threat to confiscate her costly scientific instrument.

Why would the government or the medical

establishment care whether Dr. Renee used a darkfield microscope? She speculated that the medical establishment doesn't want patients looking at their own blood under ultra-magnification because they'd see all the junk floating in it — such as undigested fragments of prescription drugs, parasites, spirochetes, and slime mold.

Case study: Patient was given 30 days to live!

In 1996 a cancer patient named Pam Woolen came to Dr. Renee's clinic and had to lie down on the clinic's floor for lack of strength. She had ovarian cancer with metastasis to the liver, and her doctor had given her only 30 days to live.

Dr. Renee turned Pam's cancer around, which inspired her, too, to become a naturopathic doctor. Today Dr. Pam Woolen is in private practice in Monroe, Wisconsin.

Sadly, conventional doctors ignore the underlying problems that cause cancer and focus ONLY on the symptom: the cancer itself.

Jim had bone cancer and was sinking fast

Back in 1993, Jim M., a 61-year-old carpenter from Chicago, got the bad news: he had prostate cancer. The doctor's solution was simple: "We take it out!" So his doctor rushed him onto an operating table to remove his prostate.

Jim was O.K. for the next nine years, but the doctor kept him on prescription drugs. The doctor still monitored Jim's PSA score to make sure the cancer was gone. By 2002, Jim's PSA was starting to rise — a bad sign. He developed a low-grade fever, for which he took antibiotics. He was losing weight. Jim describes his alarming condition: "I was sinking and sinking and sinking."

The low-grade fever lasted months. His doctor referred him to an oncologist, who gave him various drugs and injections, but Jim continued to lose weight. It turned out that bone cancer was attacking him from head to toe.

Jim's two ugliest visible tumors were on his forehead and on his inner thigh, near his knee. But he had other tumors as well.

A specialist recommended that he start chemotherapy right away.

Jim's daughter tells her Dad, "Chemo? NO WAY!"

But that's when Jim's daughter stepped in and said "NO WAY!" She'd heard of a lady in Wisconsin who'd helped someone get healed of diabetes using natural, holistic methods. She insisted that her Dad go to Wisconsin to see the lady, saying, "If it doesn't work, you can still have the chemotherapy."

So Jim went up to see Dr. Renee. She told him his cancer was grave, but she also gave him hope: "I don't heal. You'll heal yourself if you do what I tell you. But if you don't change your lifestyle, you'll be dead within months."

Jim got the message loud and clear. He followed the program to the letter.

Jim had asked a conventional doctor about a mole on his leg and was told, "It's O.K." But Dr. Renee told him, "It's *not* O.K. *It's got to go!*" The mole was actually cancer trying to erupt from his body. Dr. Renee gave him an herb to put on the mole to draw the cancer out.

A tumor the size of a fist comes out of Jim's leg!

The big tumor on Jim's leg was like an octopus. As it began shrinking, he could feel the tumor's tentacles pulling loose from his groin to his ankle. Then one day when he was at home, the tumor just came out of his leg. It was the size of his fist. This left a hole in his leg "big enough to drop a jumbo egg into," says Jim.

But within a few days — without surgery — the hole closed up! Incredible as it sounds, the skin came back together and healed naturally, leaving a fresh new layer of skin.

The healing, regenerative power of the human body never ceased to amaze Dr. Renee.

The same thing happened to the ugly tumor on Jim's forehead. Because he followed Dr. Renee's program, it just came out naturally, with no surgery whatsoever, and the hole filled in naturally with a fresh new layer of skin.

Jim made a commitment to make permanent lifestyle changes, especially dietary changes. As Dr. Renee told him, if he ever goes back to his old eating habits, his cancer will come back *with a vengeance!* That's because the body has a sort of "memory" of the cancer. And when the body's environment returns to its previous state, cancer gets the message that it's welcome to come back.

Parasites and cancer are linked

Dr. Renee put Jim through a program that cleansed the major organs of his body of toxins and eradicated his parasites. Parasites and cancer thrive in a weak, sickly, polluted body.

Dr. Renee taught her patients that parasites, such as the common roundworm, hookworm, whipworm, pinworm, and heart worm, are unbelievably easy to pick up. Depending on the type of parasite, you can get them from food or water, from mosquitoes, or through the nose or skin. Some parasites are easily visible with the naked eye; others are microscopic.

To get at the root of Jim's health problems, Dr. Renee started with his colon, putting him through a rigorous program of colon cleansing. That's because death often begins in the colon. So for 70 days straight Jim underwent colonic hydrotherapy.

After that, Dr. Renee said it was O.K. to scale his colonics back to every other day for a while. Instead of getting colonic treatments from a professional, Jim bought a colema board. This enabled him to do his colonic treatments in the privacy of his own bathroom at home — a significant saving.

A professional colonic hydrotherapy session costs from $50 to $100, depending on where you live. But Jim's colema board cost him $250, and with proper care it lasts a lifetime.

You might find this hard to believe, but Dr. Renee said that someone with a digestive tract and colon in tiptop shape will have a bowel movement about 30 minutes after each meal. That's three eliminations a day. Once a day isn't enough.

According to Dr. Renee, the reason most Americans eliminate only once a day — or less — is the typical American diet, which causes the colon to become sluggish and lazy.

She maintained that the most effective way to get the colon back in shape is through colonic hydrotherapy, a parasite cleansing program, and a healthy eating plan.

How to get rid of the unmentionable cause of cancer

Shocking as it may sound, Dr. Renee said the typical American is carrying parasites. Unfortunately, the parasites make themselves at home after entering us. Parasites, too, have to eliminate their waste, so they excrete substances that poison our bodies.

They can migrate from the colon to the various organs of the body and into the blood. Getting rid of parasites isn't a simple matter. It takes about three months because of the parasites' reproductive cycle.

The absolute best and most reliable way to get rid of parasites is to work with a knowledgeable holistic doctor who has experience in this area.

Food matters

Dr. Renee's nutritional counselor gave Jim strict guidelines for eating, which he followed to the letter.

Here's a brief summary of Dr. Renee's food plan:

- **BREAKFAST:** Fruits and juices (no fats, vegetables, or protein). Organic, if possible.
- **LUNCH:** Vegetables together with healthful fats such as extra-virgin olive oil or flaxseed oil (no protein). Organic, if possible.
- **SUPPER:** Protein together with vegetables (no starch or fruit). Organic, if possible.

Sweets are permitted, but no refined sugar. Honey, authentic maple syrup (not the fake stuff), and stevia are allowed because they're natural sweeteners. Carob is also allowed.

You can find more details about food combining as well as delicious recipes in two books by Lee

DuBelle: *Proper Food Combining Works: Living Testimony* and *Proper Food Combining Cookbook*.

The genius of Dr. Renee's eating plan is its simplicity: it enables the stomach to digest each meal completely before the next meal arrives. People who eat following this plan, and whose colons are in healthy shape, will have a good bowel movement about half an hour after each meal, and each elimination will feel complete.

According to many alternative doctors, that's how the colon is supposed to work. When your colon is working right, it moves the waste out of your body fast — in just hours. A sluggish colon causes ill health because the slow-moving sludge can get stuck in pockets of your colon, providing the ideal habitat for parasites. And the parasites create toxins that drag your health down.

"Death begins in the colon"

That's why Ilya Mechnikov, the Russian-born bacteriologist and 1908 Nobel Laureate, warned: "Death begins in the colon." Conversely, the return to health begins with cleansing the colon.

Besides cleansing the colon, Dr. Renee stressed the need to help the skin eliminate impurities. After all, the skin is the body's largest eliminative organ — even larger than the liver.

Like many holistic doctors, Dr. Renee recommended that people give every square inch of their skin a good, dry brushing every day — that's right, *brushing*. You can obtain the two brushes she recommended — a facial brush and a body brush — at www.BernardJensen.com. Just click on "Misc. Health Tools" and select the "Skin brush combo." At this writing, the combo costs $21.00.

Dry skin brushing exfoliates the dead skin cells, which renews the skin and helps it get rid of impurities. As an additional benefit, brushing stimulates most of the body's acupuncture points.

Dr. Renee also recommended hot-and-cold hydrotherapy. For example, she said you should always end a hot shower with a cold shower. Or if you take a sauna bath, you should end it with a cold shower to close your pores.

This hot-and-cold therapy effectively moves the blood from the extremities to the core. This movement of blood helps the healing process.

Besides these therapies, Dr. Renee showed her patients how to cleanse their livers, gallbladders, and kidneys.

Here are some other stories of patients Dr. Renee treated.

In a hushed tone, the chiropractor says, "I can't legally tell you this, but..."

In April of 2004, Judy M. from Madison, Wisconsin, learned she had an aggressive form of breast cancer. She's a high school economics teacher with 33 years of experience. Doctors gave her six months to live.

Judy's doctor got right to the point: "Meet with the surgeon IMMEDIATELY!"

The surgeon was a nice man. But as Judy looks back on the experience, she says, "Everything was rush, rush, rush: 'You've gotta move on this.' 'We've gotta get this scheduled.' 'I've got an opening in three days.'"

And so she was rushed onto the operating table for a lumpectomy.

As she was coming out of the anesthesia, she learned that the doctors weren't sure they got all the cancer out. They said they needed to open her up again right then and there! So she went under the knife for a second time on the same day.

Unbelievably, the surgeon called her again just five days later and said, "I think we got it all, but I want a safety valve because we might have missed something we couldn't detect. I suggest you be opened up again." And so he cut open her incision for a third time within a week.

Judy was supposed to undergo radiation and chemo after she healed up from the three surgeries.

She happened to mention to a chiropractor she'd worked with that she was undergoing treatment for aggressive breast cancer. The chiropractor took her aside and, in a hushed tone, said, "I can't legally tell you this, but cancer responds well to holistic treatment." He urged her to see Dr. Renee. He'd never met her, but he'd heard good things about her.

It's shocking that health care professionals like this chiropractor are gagged from telling the truth in America, a country that supposedly has freedom of speech!

"Give me three months and I'll prove you don't need chemo"

Judy took the chiropractor's advice. Dr. Renee outlined the program for her and told her, "Give me three months, and I'll prove you don't need chemo."

Judy discussed the holistic program with her family physician (not with her surgeon). He said, "That sounds fine. Give it the three months. Go for it. Just keep me informed."

After just seven weeks on the program, Judy's thermographic images proved she didn't need chemo or radiation. (Thermography is a safe, nontoxic and accurate way to detect breast cancer. It's superior to mammograms, and even FDA-approved, but the American medical establishment resists it.)

You see, wherever cancer is located, there are "roads" leading to it. These "roads" are called feeder lines. They are pathways that feed cancer. Judy's thermography showed that those feeder lines were dissolving and moving far away from where her cancer had been.

Judy didn't cancel the chemo treatment till they called her name in the waiting room to have her blood worked on. She met with the oncologist and showed him her thermographic images. She told him, "I'm not going through with the chemo."

He replied, "Good for you. If I can help in any way possible, let me know."

Judy then made an appointment with the radiologist to talk to him. She thought she owed him an explanation for why she wasn't going through with the radiation treatments.

The radiologist thumbed through her records and said, "What's up? We're a little behind here. We should be starting the radiation treatment."

Judy replied, "No. I'm here to tell you that I'm not going to do the radiation because I'm having good success with the natural approach."

Judy's radiologist blew his stack

The radiologist's face turned beet red with rage as he blew his stack! He chewed Judy out, basically calling her an idiot. He said he was going to call all the doctors involved in her surgery and tell them she'd chosen the WRONG path and that he was going to get her back on the *right* one.

After yelling and screaming at her for a while, he calmed down a little and said, "Look, we all need good nutrition, but it can't heal anybody. Nutrition isn't going to work. You're going to be dead in a couple of months if you don't get on the radiation table as soon as possible. You're not walking out of this building till we've got you scheduled."

It's worth noting that the radiologist gave her that warning five years ago and that Judy is still alive and free of cancer.

Then he told Judy, "We're going out to the main desk to schedule an appointment *right now!*"

He got up out of his chair, and so did Judy. The two of them walked toward the receptionist's desk. It was a Friday, and Judy was weary after a solid week of teaching. The radiologist had beaten her down. She didn't have enough fight left in her to resist his bullying.

But providentially, the phone rang. The radiologist told Judy, "You walk out to the receptionist's desk. I have to answer this call." She walked out to the desk, but no one was behind it. So she kept walking all the way to her car, then drove away. She never did submit to radiation.

Some doctors threaten, some offer support

The radiologist was furious to discover that Judy had walked out on him. So he made good on his threat to contact all of her doctors to tell them she was a foolish, disobedient, and uncooperative patient.

When Judy's surgeon received the radiologist's bad report, he mailed her a certified letter requiring her signature. The letter solemnly warned her that without radiation and chemo, "you have an unacceptably high chance for recurrent breast cancer." The surgeon said further, "you will almost certainly require a mastectomy."

Instead of trusting her radiologist and surgeon, Judy took responsibility for her health. Thank God, not all conventional doctors are as closed-minded as her radiologist and surgeon. Her family doctor and chemotherapy doctor supported her courageous decision to refuse conventional treatment.

Judy says that following Dr. Renee's program was tough, but it was *easy* on her body. She added, "Taking chemo and radiation would have been easy, but they're hard on your body."

Executive rams his golf cart into a tree — Because of a deadly form of brain cancer

On Sunday, July 23, 2006, Stewart D. was playing golf with his wife and some friends. Stewart is a 58-year-old executive with a Milwaukee foundry.

Unexpectedly, he rammed his cart right into a tree and bounced out of it onto the grass. Doctors in the foursome behind him saw what happened and came over to help. They asked, "Are you O.K.? What happened?"

Stewart told them, "I didn't see it. But I'm O.K." They told him he wasn't O.K. and needed to get to the emergency room right away. A CAT scan and an MRI revealed an unidentified mass on the right occipital lobe of his brain.

The doctors would've wheeled him into surgery the next morning, but they had to wait a week so he could wean himself off the prescription drug he was taking. The surgery took place on July 23, 2006. The surgeons discovered that the unidentified mass was glioblastoma multiforme — a deadly and fast-growing form of brain cancer.

After the operation Stewart went home for four weeks. Then he started six weeks of radiation and chemo, followed by four weeks of rest.

A friend tells him about Dr. Renee

During those four weeks, a friend asked him what he was doing about his brain cancer. The friend told him, "You need to talk to this lady near Madison."

Stewart took his friend's advice and saw Dr. Renee. He never went back for his next round of chemo or radiation. The whole process of natural healing fascinated him. He told me he feels great. His last two MRIs were negative. And he has lost more than 30 pounds — an unexpected benefit of following the program.

Regarding Dr. Renee's program, Stewart's radiation oncologist told Stewart, "They never taught us any of this in medical school." But his chemotherapy doctor took a different view: he was miffed that Stewart wouldn't undergo the next round of chemo.

Stewart remains positive. He's confident that his glioblastoma multiforme will never come back as long as he maintains his permanent lifestyle changes.

A nurse who'd seen too many patients die from cancer *treatments*

Eve W., a nurse from central Wisconsin, noticed a dark vaginal discharge in May, 2004. Tests revealed she had ovarian cancer with metastasis to the liver. Her doctors recommended surgery, radiation, and chemotherapy. They scheduled her for surgery.

But she didn't buy their recommendations. She refused surgery.

Having seen too many cancer patients die from surgery, radiation, and chemo, Eve had always said that if she ever got cancer, she'd try an alternative treatment. That time had now come.

Eve heard about an alternative clinic in Windsor, Wisconsin, and decided to go there. Dr. Renee saw Eve the same day she called because she knew cancer patients need hope and assurance.

Dr. Renee told Eve and her husband that she was seriously ill. Because Eve had been able to go about her normal activities, she hadn't fully realized how sick she was. She received instructions about lifestyle changes and went home to follow the program.

When she returned for a follow-up visit 10 days later, it was obvious her health was improving. And her health was even better 21 days later at her next follow-up visit.

After three months on the program, Dr. Renee assured her she was completely healthy. But Eve wanted even more proof the cancer was gone, so she went back to her doctors for conventional testing. When the test came back, it proved she was indeed free of cancer.

Upon reviewing her amazing recovery, one of Eve's doctors remarked, "I don't know how to treat you with diet. We weren't taught that in medical school."

A deadly brain cancer strikes a 36-year-old woman

One day in 2002, Kris S., a 36-year-old woman from Oshkosh, Wisconsin, was having a stressful day at work. Suddenly she experienced a seizure. Paramedics revived her and rushed her to the emergency room. After examination and testing, she was diagnosed with oligoastrocytoma, a nasty form of brain cancer.

On September 2, 2002, she underwent surgery. The surgeon thought he got it all, but cancer cells too small for the surgeon to see are often left behind.

Then in January, 2003, Kris suffered another seizure. The tumor had grown back, and fluid was building up in her brain. To relieve the pressure, doctors put in a shunt to drain the excess fluid. They told her that a follow-up course of chemotherapy would buy her some time.

Kris's husband wasn't happy about what the doctors were saying, and began looking for an alternative. He learned about Dr. Renee, whose clinic was a 90-minute drive from Oshkosh.

On February 3, 2003, Kris saw Dr. Renee for the first time. The doctor gave it to her straight: the good, the bad, and the ugly. Kris says it was mostly ugly because her cancer was severe. If she followed the program, she'd live. She'd have to do the work.

As for the shunt in her brain, Dr. Renee told her, "Kris, you've got to get that out now. That's a foreign object." Kris had doctors remove the shunt. She also went off all drugs, even anti-seizure medications. Instead, she went on nutritional supplements, radically changed her diet, and did the recommended cleanses.

"Everything Dr. Renee told me would happen, happened. It's a miracle I'm alive," Kris told me. She has remained cancer-free ever since her first 90 days on Dr. Renee's program, back in 2003.

Dr. Renee Welhouse suddenly dies in collision with semitrailer

As we were going to press a previous version of this book some years ago, we got the shocking news that Dr. Renee had suddenly died at the age of 57. It happened on Wednesday, March 7, 2007. At 10:35 a.m. while driving to her clinic, her car collided with a semitrailer. Emergency personnel rushed her to the University of Wisconsin Hospital in Madison, where she died shortly before noon.

All of Dr. Renee's patients and coworkers were stunned and heartbroken. Their grief was beyond words. Everyone who knew her felt a deep and irreplaceable loss. But fortunately she had taught all of her health secrets, therapies, and methods to a trusted colleague who carries on her work today, Dr. Donna Abfall, N.D., R.N.

Dr. Donna has her own amazing story of recovery from chronic, debilitating disease, an experience that explains why she has such a burning desire to help others get well.

When Donna was 10, doctors removed her tonsils and adenoids. When she didn't regain her health after surgery, they did tests to see what was wrong. They found no answer. For the next two and a half years she went to school half days because she lacked the strength to attend full days. Her immune system was practically wiped out, and she suffered migraines.

Car crash: Donna hit at 60 miles per hour

Then at age 20, Donna was in a devastating car accident: she was hit at 60 miles an hour. The crash aggravated her fragile health, triggering chronic fatigue syndrome, which turned into fibromyalgia. These health problems came on top of her earlier problems, which doctors had never solved.

Despite her health handicaps, Donna became an operating room assistant in 1979. And, with difficulty, this courageous young woman went back to school and finished her nursing studies in 1986, becoming a Registered Nurse (R.N.). Attending classes was a struggle because it was hard for her to sit in a chair long enough to make it through a class.

By 30, Donna was married with two children. Then she came down with a lung infection. A doctor gave her two antibiotics, which only gave her constant migraines. Later she got sick with an enlarged thyroid. Her chronic fatigue syndrome and fibromyalgia made her bedridden. By this time she had four children.

Drug nightmare causes Donna to quit drugs for good

A doctor gave her a drug for her migraines, which paralyzed her and caused her mind to race. She says, "It's one of the most frightening experiences I've ever had." And that's when Donna decided to never take another drug again — EVER!

She'd tried conventional medicine and was through with it. Instead, she decided to turn to a naturopathic doctor she'd heard about, Dr. Renee Welhouse. When she first saw Dr. Renee in 1998, Donna was in her late 30s and had been virtually bedridden for about ten years.

Dr. Renee tells Donna, "You're a toxic, hormonal mess!"

It took only a brief exam for Dr. Renee to see the obvious, which had stumped all of Donna's conventional doctors. She looked Donna in the eye and told her, "You're a toxic, hormonal mess!" Donna replied, "Thank you." At last, she'd found someone who saw the problem and knew the answer!

Donna went through Dr. Renee's rigorous detoxification program. During this process, Donna was so impressed with her measurable results that she decided to go to school and become a naturopathic doctor herself.

She got her N.D. degree in 2001 and began her internship with Dr. Renee in April of that year. Dr. Renee taught Dr. Donna all of her health secrets over a four-year period.

In 2005 Dr. Donna studied darkfield microscopy under Dr. Robert Bradford at the Bradford Institute in Chula Vista, California. The legendary Dr. Bradford is the same man who taught Dr. Renee darkfield microscopy.

What caused Donna's childhood illness that stemmed from the tonsillectomy? Dr. Donna suspects that a contaminated needle might have given her Epstein-Barr Syndrome, which is similar to chronic fatigue syndrome. After decades of sickness and misery, she got her health back and has remained in a vibrant state of health.

Dr. Donna is passionate about providing patients with the same level of care, compassion, and empathy they received from Dr. Renee while she was still alive. When Dr. Renee's clinic closed following her death, Dr. Donna bought the clinic's equipment and moved it into her Inochi Wellness Center in West Bend, which is about about 45 minutes from Milwaukee.

To provide her patients with a full-range of holistic medical options, including intravenous nutritional therapy, Dr. Donna works with three open-minded MDs at a medical clinic not far from West Bend. It's always a joy for Dr. Donna to see Dr. Renee's former patients in her clinic because they have an instant connection and rapport.

Contact information:

Dr. Donna Abfall, N.D. (Personally trained by the late Dr. Renee Welhouse, N.D.)
Inochi Wellness Center
2410 S Main St, Suite 109
West Bend, WI 53095
Phone: 888-864-4555
Website: www.InochiInc.com

Chapter Seventeen

Dr. Keith Block's comprehensive treatment program combines alternative and conventional medicine

By Larry Trivieri, guest author

Publisher's note: We include this chapter by our colleague Larry Trivieri because the author and co-author of this Special Report were unable to visit Dr. Block's clinic.

Integrative cancer care

In the last few years, this term has become the new catch phrase used by many oncologists and cancer treatment centers looking to capitalize on the public's growing interest in alternative cancer treatments.

In laymen's terms it's called the "best of both worlds" approach.

Unfortunately, few so-called integrative oncologists do more than give lip service to alternative approaches. They may advise their cancer patients to eat more vegetables and take a vitamin supplement, but for the most part the care they offer is still the same "one-size fits all" approach of chemotherapy, radiation, and surgery.

There are, however, a few oncologists who do truly recognize the value of natural and alternative approaches for treating cancer. In the forefront of this true integrative cancer care movement is cancer specialist Keith I. Block, M.D., co-founder and medical-scientific director of the Block Center for Integrative Cancer Treatment in Evanston, Illinois.

Not only is Dr. Block a pioneer in the field of integrative medicine, he is also the first community physician to make *chronomodulated chemotherapy* available to cancer patients in the United States.

You're probably asking, "What on earth is that?" Practiced in Europe by over 40 large centers, the emerging field of chronomodulated chemotherapy, or *chronotherapy*, represents a breakthrough use of chemotherapy that significantly minimizes chemotherapy's normal side effects, making it far more effective than conventional chemotherapy treatments.

In this chapter, you'll discover why Dr. Block's approach to treating cancer so often succeeds even in cases where conventional care has failed.

Meet Dr. Block

"Keith Block, M.D., is perhaps the most prominent integrative cancer specialist in the country."

That's the opinion of Ralph W. Moss, Ph.D., a leading author and consultant on cancer treatments.

Dr. Block has become to cancer care what Dean Ornish, M.D., is to the field of cardiovascular care – a highly regarded bridge-builder between conventional and alternative medicine.

Since the late 1970's, when he began exploring nutrition as a cancer treatment and as a component of both non-invasive and conventional therapies,

Dr. Block has treated thousands of cancer patients. He believes that blending conventional treatments with scientifically sound alternatives substantially improves quality of life – and in some cases may be the only way to keep patients alive.

Dr. Block maintains a hope-oriented, life-affirming approach to patient care and brings to his practice an impressive scientific background with thirty years of clinical experience. The combination has yielded some outstanding clinical results that have been studied and recorded over two-and-a-half decades by Dr. Block and his staff.

You don't have to wait years for the latest discoveries

As he puts it, "Our program is in a perpetual state of evolution. We monitor our patients' reactions to every part of our program, and modify it accordingly. We also act on new scientific data in real time to give patients the benefit of every relevant advance, in contrast to the years it often can take for fresh knowledge to trickle down for patient care."

Dr. Block graduated from the University of Miami College of Medicine and was an extern at London University's St. Mary Abbott Hospital in England, Chemistry and Drug Research Laboratory in Gainesville, FL, and the Veterans Administration Hospital in Gainesville, FL. He completed a residency at Illinois Masonic Medical Center, an affiliate of the University of Illinois.

Highly regarded as a medical educator, Dr. Block currently holds a number of clinical appointments, including Director of Integrative Medical Education, College of Medicine, University of Illinois at Chicago. He is also Clinical Assistant Professor, Department of Medical Education, and is the course coordinator of the "Complementary, Alternative and Integrative Medicine" Special Topics Seminar. In addition, he is an Adjunct Assistant Professor of Pharmacognosy, Department of Medicinal Chemistry and Pharmacognosy, College of Pharmacy, University of Illinois at Chicago.

Dr. Block is also a prolific researcher who directs a clinical and research staff while maintaining an active global search for the most up-to-date developments in the field of cancer care. Almost unbelievably, on top of all this he's the editor-in-chief of the peer-reviewed medical journal *Integrative Cancer Therapies,* and is on the editorial board of the *NCI/PDQ Complementary and Alternative Medicine (CAM)* at the National Cancer Institute in Bethesda, Maryland.

In short, Dr. Block is a highly accomplished physician whose approach to treating cancer cannot be dismissed by the cancer establishment for being "unproven." In fact, the Block Center is one of the few community cancer centers in the country that is deeply committed to producing clinical studies of its integrative system. What follows is a sampling of the research that Dr. Block and his colleagues have conducted.

Breast cancer patients survived twice as long with Dr. Block's approach

Dr. Block and his research team concluded a study of 90 metastatic breast cancer patients treated with chemotherapy at the Block Center whose metastases were diagnosed before 1997. The study included every single one of Dr. Block's patients with metastatic breast cancer that was treated at his clinic throughout the time of the study. The results weren't tilted toward patients who might be likely to have favorable outcomes.

Such biasing could occur by removing those with more advanced disease. It is standard practice for clinical trials to exclude patients whose conditions are more severe, the assumption being that such patients could not be helped anyway. This form of exclusion tends to artificially inflate the survival estimates. Again, this was not the case in Block's study, where all patients were included in the data. In other words, Block has taken considerable care to report his results more conservatively than accepted professional standards require.

All patients in the study received chemotherapy as part of the comprehensive, integrated Block program and were also supported by tailored supplement programs designed to improve their response to conventional drug treatment.

The median survival for Dr. Block's patients with breast cancer was *twice* that of patients who received only conventional chemotherapy.

And wait till you hear about the prostate results...

Block Program Advanced Prostate Cancer Survival Study

Dr. Block's team conducted a similar study of his prostate cancer patients, with equally impressive results. All of these 27 prostate patients had prostate cancer that had metastasized and spread to other parts of their bodies. They were treated at Dr. Block's center from 1987 to 1993, and received hormone therapy along with the full Block cancer program.

Dr. Block's study showed that the median survival rate for this group of his patients is, again, *better than twice* what usually is expected for men with metastatic prostate cancer.

Several additional comparison studies conducted by Dr. Block and his research staff divided their prostate patients into two groups, those with minimal disease or severe disease, as determined by the location of their metastases.

In regard to both the severe and minimal groups, survival rates for Dr. Block's patients were double those of patients who received conventional therapy without the benefit of the Block program. Five-year and even 10-year survivals were twice the rates seen in patients receiving only conventional therapy.

Block Program Colon Cancer Study

Finally, Dr. Block and his research group looked at colon cancer patients. A special feature of Dr. Block's therapeutic approach to metastatic colon cancer is chronotherapy, the use of a new chemotherapy delivery system that optimizes timing of drug doses.

Many patients come to the Block Center because they have not been able to tolerate needed chemotherapy due to serious side effects. Dr. Block assessed a series of patients who were unable to tolerate therapy for colon cancer. These patients were then given exactly the same chemotherapy regimens using his specialized chronotherapy pumps that are imported from Europe. Using the pumps, patients were able to better tolerate their recommended chemotherapy – with only minimal side effects – and their survival also appeared longer than usual for patients on these chemo regimens.

A program that combines alternative and conventional approaches, tailored to the individual

Dr. Block recognizes that cancer is a unique disease that cannot be treated successfully by the "magic bullet" approach that's typical of Western medicine. Sadly, there is no magic bullet that knocks out cancer, because cancer is a moving target.

"Unlike other diseases, cancer has the ability to co-opt any of the body's systems and resources to its own purpose. It can use the body's own pathways to migrate, and can divert valuable energy to stay alive. The longer cancer remains in the body, the more capable it becomes of subverting the body's life systems and protective mechanisms," Dr. Block says.

In his view, if you want to beat cancer, you need to make use of multiple therapies and techniques in an integrated approach.

Integration: The Block program is designed to restore the body's biological integrity with the aim of stopping cancer's takeover. This is accomplished by integrating the best tools that both conventional and alternative medicine have to offer. The program involves first restoring balance to his patients' everyday lives, including their diet, physical fitness levels, their psychological and social well-being, and their surrounding home and work environment.

Then, the program focuses on restoring balance to the patients while making their micro-environment inhospitable to cancer. To achieve this goal, Dr. Block pioneered a comprehensive system that he uses along with analyses of six aspects of the body's internal environment that he calls "terrain factors", such as inflammation, oxidation, stress chemistry and other characteristics.

This comprehensive set of assessments allows Dr. Block and his staff to custom tailor restorative treatment plans that meet the specific needs of each of his patients.

Dr. Block likes to remind his patients that each area of the Block program depends on and reinforces the others, so any step taken in the right direction can have a positive ripple effect over the entire system.

Individualization: The other distinguishing focus of the Block program is its core emphasis on *individualization*. No two patients in Dr. Block's clinic are on precisely the same program. The reason Dr. Block gives for this is simple: no two patients are precisely the same, even if they have been given the same diagnosis at the same stage in life.

As mentioned above, Dr. Block sees cancer as a disease that profits from imbalance anywhere it occurs. Types of imbalance include: poor nutrition, an unhappy relationship, an unhealthy physical environment, biochemical imbalances in the body, side effects of conventional cancer therapy or genetic predisposition. Each patient's particular set of strengths and vulnerabilities is unique, so the doctor has to design a system of care to match that unique pattern and compensate for its weaknesses.

"For cancer, there is no such thing as one size fits all," Dr. Block explains. "That's why we've put so much energy into developing the assessment tools we use for our patients. And like other aspects of our program, our assessments are continuously reviewed to embrace new clinical and scientific findings."

High-level assessments make unique individualized programs possible

The purpose of Dr. Block's full diagnostic program is to better target and tailor the use of a group of therapeutic tools that he and his staff have honed over many years of experience.

Supplements are one of the fundamental aspects of the Block program. Block uses supplements, nutraceuticals and superfoods to further the goals of the patient's overall program. The first step in individualizing supplement recommendations is a series of assessments recommended for all of Dr. Block's patients.

Dr. Block explains the value of these tests as follows: "Unless we know one's biological condition and what specific areas of weakness exist, we cannot tailor a program to suit a patient's specific needs. Plus, attending to our assessments helps serve as an early warning system. These tests help us catch a tumor on the rise before it gets out of hand."

The comprehensive set of assessments covers all aspects of his patients' lives, including their social and spiritual support networks, eating habits, physical fitness, body composition analysis, internal biochemistry, type of disease, tumor tissue profiling and their level and type of daily physical activity.

For example, Dr. Block recalls one patient who needed to talk about his professional life at the beginning of every visit before it was possible for him to discuss his disease. But Dr. Block was prepared for this dynamic because he had conducted and reviewed the patient's personal priorities assessment. After months of this patient's bouncing from doctor to doctor and avoiding treatment, the insight gained from a psychological assessment allowed Dr. Block to help him get serious about addressing his disease.

Some of the assessments are used to identify individual strengths as well as the unique challenges each person faces in coping with cancer. Explaining why these assessments are important, Dr. Block cites studies that show anxiety and depression often go under-detected in cancer patients.

Why does this matter? Because convincing studies suggest that *hopelessness* is linked to an increased death rate from cancer. Dr. Block believes that only by employing highly sensitive diagnostics can the caregiver learn the individual nature of these damaging conditions.

In the physical wellness evaluation, Dr. Block and his staff include body composition analysis (BCA) to measure the ratio of muscle to fat in patients so they can better monitor the risks of any changes in weight over the course of the disease.

"One of the biggest mistakes," says Dr. Block "is thinking that any weight loss in a cancer patient is a bad sign. I can show you many patients who may lose weight, but add muscle mass. This is actually a good thing, because being overweight is associated with increased mortality, while maintaining muscle mass, using tailored exercise along with specific muscle-maintaining supplements, is the surest way to avoid the onset of wasting, or cachexia."

Dr. Block's team also determines appropriate nutrition for each patient, based on the state of his or her digestive system.

In addition, Dr. Block's staff tests each patient for endurance, recovery capacity, and aerobic competence, strength and flexibility. Each of these is connected to a person's ability to adapt to physical or other stresses. "Adapt to stress" has a specific, scientific meaning here. It means the ability to return to a normal state after exposure to stress. And it's been linked directly to death rates from all types of disease.

Dr. Block's clinic runs lab tests for stress hormones to evaluate each patient, since stress hormone levels are associated with the prognosis – the outlook for recovery – for cancer patients.

Dr. Block and his research team have also developed a sophisticated panel of nutritional tests at both the macro and micro level of nutrition. They test for albumin level, blood proteins, and the micronutrient status of a number of different nutrients and phytochemicals that have anticancer effects.

Some examples of such nutrients include vitamins A, E and C, beta carotene, alpha carotene, lutein, lycopene, CoQ10, and three different types of B vitamins. Depending on a patient's circumstances, the Block Clinic also examines the ratios between omega-3 and omega-6 fatty acids. Improvements in these fatty acid ratios can favorably influence tumor response, reduce resistance of the tumor cells to chemotherapy, and lead to longer survival for patients with advanced cancers.

Patients also receive a full panel of immune system tests, to measure immune system cells and biochemicals such as lymphocytes, the activity of natural killer (NK) cells, and other immune system chemicals and cells.

The physicians at his center often utilize chemosensitivity testing on fresh tissue biopsied from a patient's tumor. By testing the chemotherapy drugs against cancer cells cultured from a patient's tumor, this tissue assessment can improve the odds of choosing the most effective chemotherapeutic agent for each patient.

Fighting cancer with tools of the mind and spirit

Once Dr. Block and his team decide on an individualized treatment plan for each patient, the mind-spirit staff at the Block Center teaches patients a set of self-calming techniques that are personalized to match each person's needs and individual style.

This is an important aspect of the Block Center's overall approach to treating cancer, since chronic, unrelieved stress is one contributing factor to cancer and most other illnesses.

Ultimately, the goal of this component of the Block program is to enable patients to regain their interest in enjoying life and assert a sense of control over their lives. Many of Dr. Block's patients report that their experiences with cancer at the Block Center gave them a new sense of purpose and meaning in their lives that goes far beyond their short term need to cope with their illness.

A three-part program to strengthen the body

The physical care component of the Block program has three parts. The first is a daily basic routine that consists of a series of stretches and movements.

The second part is a core conditioning regimen. It's designed to build strength and endurance, increase vitality, and help the patient adapt to stress.

The third component is supportive body care, which can include acupressure, massage, and neuromuscular therapy.

Each of these three areas benefits the patient physically by increasing oxygen flow to cells and tissues (cancer cells have a difficult time existing in an oxygen-rich environment), building and maintenance of lean muscle mass, and enhancing natural killer (NK) cell activity.

The Block physical care program also enhances the body's ability to detoxify – to get rid of poisonous substances. Most of Dr. Block's patients report that his physical care regimen helps them ease feelings of depression and anxiety.

Fighting cancer with good, nutritious food

Dr. Block has been advising patients for decades to follow a diet based chiefly on phytochemical-rich vegetables and fruits – including broccoli, tomatoes, and blueberries, excellent sources of glucosinolates, lycopene and proanthocyanidins – and whole unprocessed grains.

The diet also features protein sources such as fish, soy, and other legumes, all containing healthier fats than those found in animal-based products such as meat and dairy. Patients are advised to eat few sweets, and those they do eat should be low-glycemic. Highly glycemic foods enter the blood as pure sugar very quickly after being eaten, and cancer cells thrive on sugar.

The Block team has developed over the years what Dr. Block calls "the Superfood Group." This is a core supplemental program of food concentrates designed to supply all patients with the vital nutrients they need. Without the supplements they may fail to obtain these nutrients.

The first element of the superfood group, aptly named Turbogreens, is a highly concentrated powdered extract of vegetables grown on an organic farm. The second superfood, Whey and Berry with Flax, is a combination of ingredients and compounds shown to have impressive anticancer value. The third superfood is Dr. Block's researched Arctic fish oil.

The fourth superfood is Fiberboost. It helps improve bowel regularity and reduce the binding of toxins while supporting the health of the bowel lining or wall.

Common multivitamins may help PROMOTE tumor growth

Dr. Block raises concerns that general multiple-vitamin or mineral pills found in the marketplace contain compounds that may promote tumor growth. Thus, his fifth superfood is a concentrated multivitamin and antioxidant preparation tailored to the needs of cancer patients by removing cancer promoting compounds while adding specific adaptogenic herbs and phytochemicals (nutrients found in plants).

The biochemically-focused supplements Dr. Block prescribes are designed to help patients achieve optimal levels in seven biochemical markers associated with cancer onset, progression, and recurrence. For example, one agent called Mycoessentials contains immune stimulating components extracted from six exotic mushrooms.

Dr. Block and the center's research team have also spent a great deal of time perfecting groupings of natural agents designed to counteract the nasty side effects of certain cancer treatments. As a result, based on surveys performed at the clinic, Block Center patients suffer far less than average patients from side effects common with most chemotherapy protocols

New, innovative treatments: fractionated infusion and chronotherapy

The Block Center administers conventional cancer treatments in unique, gentle ways, with the goal of reducing or eliminating the toxic side effects they so often cause. "Chemotherapy, radiation, and surgery can be extremely harsh on the body," Dr. Block says. "Not only do they have direct negative effects on immunity, but often the body becomes overly toxic and malnourished as a result of the treatment." To help protect his patients from these negative effects, Dr. Block has incorporated two innovative approaches for using chemotherapy: fractionated infusion and chronotherapy.

Fractionated Infusion: For decades, Dr. Block and his clinical team have been using fractionated infusion when administering chemotherapy. This means that instead of receiving one large, highly toxic hit of chemotherapy drugs, a patient receives smaller dosages over a longer period of time. Although this takes longer than the traditional dose, the toxicity to the patient is significantly reduced and more easily tolerated.

When fractionated dosing is coupled with exercise and a set of relaxation practices, the reduction in side effects can be truly remarkable. Dr. Block is fond of telling how one patient strapped his special chemo pump into a fanny pack and rollerbladed down a ten-mile path along the shore of Lake Michigan each day while receiving his chemotherapy. Not only did this patient get great aerobic exercise, which helps fight his cancer, he virtually eliminated the side effects of the drug he was taking.

Chronotherapy: Another way Dr. Block reduces unwanted effects of conventional treatments is through the process called chronotherapy, or chronomodulated chemotherapy mentioned at the beginning of this chapter.

As Dr. Block's website explains, "Chronotherapy is based on the scientific fact that our biochemistry behaves differently at different times of the day. This series of 24-hour cycles are commonly referred to as the body's circadian rhythms. Chronotherapy seeks to exploit this fact by calibrating the dosing of chemotherapy agents to these circadian rhythms.

By honoring the body's circadian rhythm, chronotherapy is better able to optimize the effectiveness of chemotherapy drugs while simultaneously reducing their toxic side effects.

"The benefits of putting time on the side of the patient cannot be overstated," Dr. Block says. He first began using chronotherapy in 1997. "I initially brought this technology to the U.S. in order to help our patients better tolerate their chemotherapy treatments but am equally impressed by its ability to improve treatment response and impact patient survivals."

The scientific data in support of chronotherapy is plentiful, and yet the Block Center is the only private clinic in the United States that has incorporated it into their treatment of patients. In fact, studies show that if chronotherapy is administered correctly, it can almost double the ten-year survival rate. Better yet, with some cancers, including ovarian cancer, it can multiply the five-year survival rate four times over, compared to patients given the same drug without the benefits of chronotherapy.

Dr. Block also tries to strengthen his patients' internal biochemistry to better protect against toxic effects of treatment. All his patients receive intravenous nutrients and chemotherapy simultaneously. This helps patients retain proper levels of certain micronutrients that can help them tolerate treatment, but which are usually destroyed during chemotherapy. When these vital micronutrients are missing, side effects can result.

Dr. Block also employs a combination of ten herbs derived from the Chinese Fu Zheng treatment approach. They've been shown for decades to help people withstand the rigors of chemotherapy and radiation. For more than a decade, Dr. Block's patients have been receiving this herbal formula in the form developed by his research team, called Anticancer Botanical Agents, or ACBA.

Helping the body detoxify

The Block Center provides two types of detoxification for its patients: one for people in remission, or those who are not currently receiving conventional treatment, and one practiced between cycles of chemotherapy or radiation. The goal of both is to rebuild and repair the body's resources by improving the body's ability to eliminate toxins.

The Block team focuses on improving all routes of toxic elimination: the skin, through brushing, sea salt baths, and therapeutic saunas; the respiratory system, with gentle breathing exercises; and the bowel and liver functions.

Dr. Block has developed four detoxification aids to be taken by mouth during the detoxification process: a botanical blend that upgrades the liver's ability to make fat soluble compounds water soluble so they're flushed out of the body more easily; a fiber product that binds toxins so they won't be reabsorbed into the body; an antioxidant that assists the colon and intestines in handling the higher than usual toxic volume; and digestive enzymes that help to break down the molecules containing toxins into pieces more easily eliminated.

Real-life patient success stories

The following case histories illustrate what is possible for cancer patients to achieve at the Block Center, even after their previous doctors have told them they were going to die.

Kidney Cancer: When G was in his early forties life was good: he was raising cattle, as several generations of his family had done before him. Although he often worked between sixteen and eighteen hours a day, seven days a week, he had the sense of doing exactly what he wanted with his life. Not surprisingly, G's diet consisted of red meat twice a day, accompanied by a tremendous amount of milk, cheese and sweets of all kinds.

Over time, however, G found he simply couldn't keep up his grueling work schedule. At first, he became irritable and started losing weight. Then G began to feel extremely fatigued and he could feel a hard mass in his abdomen. Still, G didn't call a doctor until he passed blood in his stool. By then he had also lost 55 pounds. G says, "I was too busy to even think about it. It wasn't even in my mind that I had something seriously wrong."

A sonogram confirmed that G's kidney was about the size of a cantaloupe. When G went to a urologist the next day, he was told he had renal cell carcinoma and that the disease would respond to neither chemotherapy nor radiation. A surgery date was set for the following week.

"After the surgery I was nothing but skin and bones," G recalls. "We were all concerned about my weight being so low so I was eating everything I could get my hands on: milk shakes, ice cream and steaks. Little did we know we were feeding the cancer."

Nine months later G had metastases in his lymph nodes and his doctor told him the cancer had spread to his liver. G recalls his doctor "told me I should get my affairs in order because I had six months to live." G and his family knew something had to be done. He dug out a doctor's telephone number given to him by one of the nurses who cared for him when he had his kidney removed. She had told him that her father had the same illness as G, and with the help of the doctor whose number she wrote down, he had survived it. That doctor was Dr. Block.

When G first met Dr. Block, what struck him most was "[Dr. Block] was very open and told us like it was. He provided us with hope. This was the first doctor that told us there was a chance. He initially asked me, 'Why did you come here?' My reply to him was, 'I want to live.' Dr. Block said that was reason enough."

Dr. Block started G on an immunotherapy drug immediately, buttressed by the Block program, and G remained under Dr. Block's supervision for two weeks until his condition stabilized.

During his stay in Chicago, another of Dr. Block's patients, D, the father of G's nurse who also suffered from kidney cancer, called G on the phone and drove out from Michigan to visit with G and offer encouragement. G remembers, "Just to see him standing in my room and knowing he had renal cell gave me hope." (At that time, D had lived seven years past his diagnosis and original prognosis of six months' survival.)

G and his family committed to his following the Block program one hundred percent. G starts every day with morning meditation and exercises on a stationary bike for a minimum of 20 minutes. He and his family make following the Block diet a group effort. With the help of Penny Block's cookbook, A Banquet of Health, preparing healthful and delicious food has become easy.

It is now eighteen years since G was told he had only six months to live. He sleeps six or seven hours a night and works twelve hours a day. He and his family go on vacation, something they never did before, and he's traded elk hunting for shooting clays.

His diet has changed drastically for the better and on the farm where once beef was raised, G and his family harvest organic produce. The eight hundred pounds of red meat G had put in his freezer just before meeting Dr. Block is still being used, little by little, for cat food, eighteen years later. And recently, G held his first grandchild in his arms, something he feared he would never live to do.

G says he approaches life one day at a time, knowing he is a survivor who has been given the "gift of life." "I just wish there were a way to tell everyone who gets cancer about this program. I have stated numerous times, 'If you want to live, call this number.' "

Metastatic Breast Cancer: M was the kind of person who never stopped. She was an exercise addict, who would begin her day by lifting weights at 5:45 a.m. for almost two hours. She worked two jobs and put 50,000 miles on her car in one year. Her diet was composed chiefly of fast food that she could grab on the road because she almost never took the time to cook.

M was in her mid-forties and appeared to be in peak physical condition when she found a large lump in her breast. Her dislike of doctors kept her from seeking help for almost six months, but once she went to see her physician, within five days of her examination M underwent a modified radical mastectomy.

At her follow-up visit, her surgeon told her "I'm sorry but you will die from this," and it was then that M's rebellious spirit was triggered. She began reading voraciously and found mention of the Block Medical Center in a book, so she decided to make an appointment.

Dr. Block performed a full assessment of M when she first arrived at Block Medical. He found that although she was in good physical condition and within normal weight range, her exercise regimen was too intense and contributed to a considerable elevation in inflammatory markers confirmed by laboratory testing. (According to Dr. Block, normal exercise routines decrease inflammation. However M's was excessive, particularly with the condition she was battling.)

M had also taken quite a rigid approach to her diet once she was diagnosed with cancer, switching to a complete macrobiotic regime. Before she ever underwent the formal psychological assessment, Dr. Block and his staff could clearly see M had considerable phobia in dealing with medical settings.

Using his biochemical markers, Dr. Block also found a serious imbalance in the level of stress hormones in her body; a higher than normal level of oxidation; a high level of inflammation from over-exercise; and a greatly reduced detoxification capacity due, at least in part, to her history as a smoker. The laboratory report from M's mastectomy was discouraging: her tumor was 4.5 centimeters in diameter. In addition, M's cancer had metastasized to ten of thirteen lymph nodes that were analyzed.

Dr. Block began a comprehensive effort to restore balance to M's life. First, he advised M to emphasize stretching and flexibility exercises as well as hiking and other organic activities and de-emphasize high impact, high inflammation routines that involved weight lifting.

Likewise, with respect to her strict macrobiotic diet, he advised her to loosen her approach, allowing herself essential nutrients such as omega-3 fatty acids found in fish oil, and lycopene, which is found in tomatoes, which are often restricted in a macrobiotic regimen.

Finally, the Block Center mind-spirit team worked intensively with M to help overcome her anxiety, recapture the pleasure in her life, and alleviate her depression. Perhaps most importantly, M learned to abandon her rigidity in regard to herself and the world. This allowed her to engage with greater ease in satisfying activities and to reframe important connections with family members, who provided support of inestimable value to M as she dealt with her disease.

Dr. Block had to break down years of mistrust of the medical community to develop a relationship with M. Then he began speaking with her about chemotherapy, which she had refused even to consider in the past. (M admits that her initial search for a physician was centered on finding someone who would not recommend conventional therapies.)

He spoke to her over a long period about some of his patients' experiences and why he felt the level of her disease made chemotherapy advisable. He told her how well patients endured the treatment when they did fractionated chemotherapy combined with his tailored nutraceutical approach, bolstered by the full Block program. Dr. Block explained that both her chemo and her supplements would be tailored to her individual circumstances and he would be sensitive to her personal values.

M agreed to start chemotherapy accompanied by Dr. Block's core supplements. She used the periodic detoxification regimen over the course of her therapy. M's cancer was very active. But so was M. She received a then common chemotherapy protocol referred to as CAF, which included Cytoxan®, Adriamycin® and 5-Fluorouracil administered through the fractionated infusion Dr. Block recommended.

With the assistance of a special portable chemotherapy unit, M put her chemo in a fanny pack and walked ten miles during each session that the drugs entered her system.

Today M is like a poster child for restored balance. Her lifestyle has been completely reformed to reflect the equal importance of work, relaxation, and relationship building. Her improved diet and exercise regimens as well as intensive psychological work and introspection has brought her to a point where she honestly says that although she would not have wished for a cancer diagnosis, "my life after cancer is richer than it was before."

M takes pride in sticking to the Block program and never missing a meal or a day of work during the whole time she undertook chemotherapy. Today, over eight years since her diagnosis and since her surgeon told her she would die of her disease, M is completely malignancy-free.

Commenting on such successes Dr. Block says, "If a patient at any time expresses a sincere desire to fight their disease and battle for their life, who am I to deny them that right – that's enough for me to pull out all the stops and begin guiding them along the road to recovery."

Contact information:

Keith Block, M.D.
Block Center for Integrative Cancer Treatment
5230 Old Orchard Road
Skokie, IL 60077
Phone: 877-41-BLOCK (877-412-5625)
Website: www.BlockMD.com

Chapter Eighteen

America's most famous alternative doctor talks about today's cancer treatment options

Julian Whitaker, M.D., is a living legend in the field of holistic medicine, or, as he calls it, "good medicine." He's the founder and director of the Whitaker Wellness Institute in Newport Beach, California, which draws patients from all over America. His newsletter, *Health and Healing,* has had more subscribers than any similar newsletter.

Dr. Whitaker was kind enough to let us interview him about cancer treatment options in America today and other health issues. And after the interview, which we've printed below, one of his employees gave us a tour of his clinic, which makes extensive use of cutting edge therapies such as hyperbaric oxygen and external counter-pulsation, as well as traditional therapies such as acupuncture.

Here's the interview with Dr. Whitaker:

Frank Cousineau: You have a vast knowledge of cancer and how to treat even the cases other doctors call "hopeless" and "terminal." What advice would you give to a cancer victim?

Dr. Whitaker: Well, let me give you my thoughts on cancer. We don't treat cancer. As a matter of fact we discourage patients with cancer from coming here. When patients with cancer do come here, we treat the patient's general health and add to the nutritional support of his or her health.

A unique cancer breakthrough

I routinely refer cancer patients to Dr. Stanislaw Burzynski in Houston. Dr. Burzynski has a unique discovery on the treatment of cancer that deals with undisciplined multiplication, which is, in my opinion, the only breakthrough in the treatment of cancer we've experienced in the last hundred years.

[Editor's note: In 1992, investigators from the National Cancer Institute visited Dr. Burzynski's clinic and examined the medical records of seven terminally ill brain cancer patients. They concluded that Dr. Burzynski's treatment caused a complete or partial remission in every case. (Reference: Hawkins, M.G., Friedman, M.A.; *Journal of the National Cancer Institute,* 1992; 84: 22, 1701) You can call the office of Stanislaw Burzynski, M.D., Ph.D., at 713-335-5697 for more information.]

There are some things I think can also be helpful. One of them is a very large dose of Vitamin C. Dr. Hugh Riordan had been doing that, I think for 20 years, in Wichita, Kansas, until he passed away a few years ago. His practice in part is now under the direction of Dr. Ron Hunninghake, the Chief Medical Officer of the Olive W. Garvey Center for Healing Arts, the clinical division of the Riordan Clinic. They are actually studying chemotherapeutic use of vitamin C. In that therapy, they infuse vitamin C and at the same time test blood levels of vitamin C to hit a level deemed to be appropriate in the treatment of cancer.

The primary reason we discourage cancer patients from coming to our own clinic is because it is such a highly politicized issue. The reason it's a highly politicized issue, in my opinion, is that conventional therapy is no more than a dangerous placebo. So when you have the death rate from cancer, and the incidence rate of cancer staying virtually the same for over a hundred years, that is the definition of a placebo: therapies that just don't work but are believed to work.

The government targets alternative cancer doctors

Yet the industry of cancer is so bolstered financially that they govern all of the other regulatory aspects of medicine to ensure that choice is not available to cancer patients except surgery, chemotherapy, and radiation. Anyone who treats cancer in this country with therapies other than surgery, radiation, and chemotherapy has put a very large red target on his back for suppression. I just don't want to do that and I don't want to live in Mexico, so we stay away from cancer for political reasons.

I believe I could be a better oncologist with natural therapies than the oncologists are now with chemotherapy. Now that's just my opinion. I will never test that opinion because I will not put myself in that kind of jeopardy.

Frank Cousineau: How did you get into what we generally call "alternative medicine"?

Dr. Whitaker: Well, I don't really like the term "alternative medicine." If we look at the term "alternative medicine" and clearly define it, alternative therapies are therapies that are not taught in medical school and not used in hospitals.

Now that's an unstable definition because virtually everything in medicine today was at one time alternative. Everything: antibiotics, hand washing, sterile technique, and so on.

However, there are certain elements, for business reasons, that are constantly excluded as medical therapies. I'm talking about natural products such as vitamins and minerals, acupuncture, or low-tech, inexpensive products that would compete for the health care dollar with large pharmaceuticals that have patented substances and/or with the high-tech approaches that are used in hospitals with surgery.

So I don't like the term "alternative medicine." I do like the term "good medicine." That's all I try to practice: good medicine. I do what I consider to be best for a patient.

The best way to define our medicine, I think, is to call it "molecular medicine." That's a term Linus Pauling coined. Molecular medicine is the use of substances that are common and essential to the body in various dosages to facilitate health and to treat disease. This includes Vitamin C, water, oxygen, hyperbaric oxygen, folic acid, magnesium, and the whole array of what we know as nutritional supplements.

These supplements have only been a part of human civilization for about 60 years; a very new source of innovation is to be able to find these active ingredients and actually put them in a dosable form. So that describes most of what we do here.

Most of the diseases we treat here are not nearly as politically charged as is cancer. We treat high blood pressure, stroke, heart disease, a lot of diabetes, obesity, and the degenerative diseases other than cancer.

Frank Cousineau: At what point did you decide that good medicine included all of the things that you just described, as opposed to what you were taught in medical school?

Dr. Whitaker: I think the major turning point was when I spent about six months on the staff of the Longevity Institute under the direction of Dr. Nathan Pritikin in 1976. He had an operation very similar to mine. People would come for a residential program in which his therapeutic tools were diet and exercise only. So it was a rigorous lifestyle intervention program, and I followed people who were on that program. And I saw people get well.

Patients who take prescription drugs aren't well

In conventional medicine, you rarely if ever see anybody get well because they're always changing drugs. They always have something that they "require" to have a prescription drug treatment for. People who are taking prescription drugs are by definition not well. That doesn't mean that everyone not taking a prescription drug is well, but if you're on a prescription drug, you're not well. You could be better, but you're not well. But when you use natural, molecular substances, your chances of creating wellness are good.

Seeing people get well solidified the direction I would take in my own medical practice. Hence, we have a residential program. This is not a hospital. Our patients stay in a hotel, but we treat them here. We educate them on lifestyle.

Frank Cousineau: Many cancer patients are also suffering from conditions such as diabetes and obesity. Could you address those conditions?

Dr. Whitaker: Yes. Now I've written a book on diabetes, and I'll give you one when you leave.

Here's how I would summarize our approach with diabetes Type I: we do everything we can to reduce the amount of insulin required to keep someone under good control. And the tools that reduce the amount of insulin required to keep someone under good control are the lifestyle. If a Type I diabetic gets involved in an exercise regimen, his insulin requirement is going to drop substantially. If a Type I diabetic gets involved in a diet that is low-glycemic and high in fiber, his insulin requirement is going to drop.

But the area where I think we are most different from conventional treatment of Type I and Type II diabetes is that we vociferously advise and prescribe and put our patients on nutritional supplements. And the reason this is such an integrated part of our treatment for diabetes is because the term diabetes means excessive urination. And "diabetes" is actually the Greek word for "passing through."

The blood sugar acts like a powerful diuretic. So when people have excessive urination, which is one of the cardinal symptoms of Type I diabetes, they are losing copious amounts of urine with sugar in it and with everything else. The sugar in the blood overwhelms the kidneys' capacity to conserve water-soluble nutrients. So the diabetic is dangerously low, almost always, in magnesium, folic acid, vitamins C, B12, zinc.

All the water soluble nutrients are washed out because the patients have a nutritional wasting phenomenon going on.

I believe that this nutritional wasting is a primary reason, if not the major reason, for diabetic complications. If you were to put someone on an osmotic diuretic daily that caused the degree of nutritional wasting that Type I diabetics do experience, you'd have the eye problems, the nerve problems, and all of the other problems that they experience just on the nutritional wasting because they waste everything. They have oxidative stress all the time, yet they peed out all their antioxidants.

So in 30 years, and with probably 25,000 diabetic patients, we have never had a single diabetic patient — either Type I or Type II — come in who has been prescribed nutritional supplements to compensate for what everyone knows is a massive loss of water-soluble nutrients because of the nature of the disease — not one. It is one of the biggest flaws I can think of.

Not to supply the diabetic with copious amounts of water-soluble and freely available and inexpensive nutrients is beyond my comprehension. Not because I believe they work, but simply because any measurement of the nutritional status of the diabetic indicates major loss. So that's the main thing.

We tell our Type I diabetics, "We will institute a variety of methods to control your blood sugar. But so do conventional doctors. However, where we really differ is that we give you extra amounts of high potency vitamins to compensate for the loss."

Why Americans weigh too much: culprit revealed

Frank Cousineau: What about obesity?

Dr. Whitaker: Well, I've just written a book on obesity, and in that book — and I'll give you one you can take with you — I point out two things. I think I've hit on the primary reason why we have a pandemic of obesity. What do you think it is?

Frank Cousineau: Diet.

Dr. Whitaker: What about the diet? What's so different now than it was in the '50s and '60s?

Frank Cousineau: It's the things that people choose to eat; it's a fast food nation; it's the lack of nutritional quality in the foods that are grown; lack of exercise; and people don't take the time to sit down and eat a good, well-balanced meal.

Dr. Whitaker: Okay. I disagree. Because everyone says either what you said or else portion size — or lack of exercise. Right? We are all trying to find why the number of people who are obese in this country has exploded by about 50 percent. I have those statistics in the book. It's an explosion, and it has only occurred in this country.

It did not occur in France; it did not occur in England; it did not occur in Italy. It has never been a problem in Asia. Why? Why is the United States so different? Other countries have fast food. England has fish and chips restaurants.

Here's the difference: In the 1970s there was a substantial shift in the country toward carbohydrates. The Senate Select Committee on Nutrition, headed by Senator George McGovern, came out with guidelines that said let's make starch a major caloric contributor. And the food industry jumped on the bandwagon and decided to vilify all fat as the reason for heart disease, obesity, and so on.

Yes, the food industry took this message to heart. And when you talk about the food industry, you don't talk about them advocating the fruits and vegetables. You talk about them coming out with nonfat Twinkies, nonfat desserts, nonfat milk, nonfat yogurts, and these types of things.

So the food industry began stripping fat and adding the calories in carbohydrate. And the nation followed, and I have those statistics in the book where the carbohydrate increase only went up about two to three percent. And the fat intake actually reduced. And if that initial belief was accurate, we should have had a reduction in weight, regardless of calorie intake. But we turned the nation into a feedlot. And by altering the food and increasing starch intake, human beings exploded. How do you fatten cattle?

Frank Cousineau: Put 'em in a pen and give 'em corn.

Dr. Whitaker: Corn. And what is corn primarily? Starch. So we're mammals. We have the same proclivities and the same chemistries, and the same metabolism of handling starch that all other mammals have that eat starch. We get fat.

Dr. Whitaker's weight loss secret: How he lost 30 pounds

I've lost about 30 pounds. I hadn't been eating at McDonald's. I wasn't on the fast food thing, but I was eating a whole bunch of bread and some dessert, and now I'm 30 pounds lighter because I just eliminate bread and eliminate dessert. And now I'm exercising more, so there's a lot to it.

When you talk to someone who's lost 70 pounds, invariably 80 percent of them will say they cut off carbohydrates. The evidence keeps slapping us in the face all the time, and we ignore it, and we say Atkins was an idiot. And yet the people who really do seriously lose weight control their starch intake.

I don't go so far as to eliminate all starches. I say eat fruit. I've never known anybody who was obese from excessive fruit consumption; [although] you probably could do it. Apples help you to lose weight because they're high in fiber. So if people will eat fruit and vegetables, but just stay off starch, they will lose weight. So that's one thing.

How to *guarantee* you'll have the discipline to lose weight

Another important factor is discipline, because few can stay on a program. They will resolve to lose weight, but they will rarely resolve to change with any kind of discipline the behaviors they need to change in order to lose weight. They say, "Well, I'm not going to eat this, I'm not going to eat that," and there will always be exceptions because there are no consequences to breaking the New Year's resolution.

In my book, I point out how you make a contract with yourself with a negative consequence if you don't follow through on your contract. And the contract has some specifics.

First, it needs to be a behavior, not a result.

Second, it needs to be time-limited so that you don't make it for the rest of your life. You can always renew.

Dr. Whitaker's ingenious punishment if he "cheats"

Third, there needs to be a significant punishment for not following through. I recommend a financial punishment. Let me tell you what my punishment is. I despise the ACLU. I think they degrade society, so I would never give them any money. So in my contract I agree not to eat breads or sugar desserts for three months. If I so much as eat any breads or sugar desserts in three months, I will send a thousand dollars to the ACLU.

Frank Cousineau: That would be a tremendous motivation.

Dr. Whitaker: It is a tremendous motivation. Then I sign it, I witness it, and I put it up on the bulletin board somewhere. We have it downstairs for people to do this. It's amazing how much discipline that can cause to bubble up, to where now it isn't a problem. You just don't do it. And one of the reasons — it's as if you had an invisible guy behind you with a baseball bat and you want to stop smoking, and you instructed him to hit you in the back of the head very hard with a baseball bat the minute you took a single puff of a cigarette. I don't care how much you want the cigarette, you are not going to take a puff as long as you know he's back there.

Frank Cousineau: Getting back to cancer, I've seen a lot of cancer patients get rid of their cancer at alternative clinics. The cancer would be gone — three weeks, three months — the cancer was under control. And then six months to a year or a year and a half later, some of these patients would die of a heart attack or stroke. I stressed this to some of the alternative clinics. I said, "You have to broaden your horizons. When you get the cancer under control, you have to follow through with what you say you're doing, and that's taking care of the whole patient."

Dr. Whitaker: Many of the people who are treating cancer using nonconventional therapies are strongly into dietary changes that I would agree with. So I think if someone is getting benefit from an alternative therapy in cancer, it is also most likely lowering the risk of other diseases as well. Because a natural approach to reduce cancer is not inherently dangerous as far as heart disease, diabetes, and anything else is concerned.

Contact information:

Julian Whitaker, M.D.
Whitaker Wellness Institute Medical Clinic, Inc.
4321 Birch Street
Newport Beach, CA 92660
Phone: 800-488-1500
Email: info@whitakerwellness.com
Website: www.whitakerwellness.com

Contact information for the cancer clinic to which Dr. Whitaker refers cancer patients who seek alternative therapy:

Stanislaw Burzynski, M.D., Ph.D.
Burzynski Clinic
9432 Katy Freeway
Houston, TX 77055
Phone: 713-335-5697
Fax: 713-935-0649
Email: info@burzynskiclinic.com
Website: www.burzynskiclinic.com

Chapter Nineteen

Armed federal goons raid one of America's top clinics: Camelot Cancer Care

The Camelot Cancer Care clinic in Tulsa, Oklahoma, earned a reputation as one of the top alternative cancer clinics in America. We toured this impressive clinic and interviewed the doctors and some patients. Unfortunately, the federal government launched a sneak attack against Camelot in a raid that effectively shut the clinic down without due process of law. At this writing, we don't know whether the shutdown is permanent or temporary.

Here's what happened. . .

On April 23rd, 2013, a group of armed federal agents dressed in plain clothes burst into the Camelot Cancer Care clinic and started poking around as if they owned the place. They presented no identification. Maureen Long, the clinic founder and director, wasn't in the clinic during the raid because she'd just undergone surgery and was recovering at home.

Maureen's right-hand-man, Michael McDonnough, however, was at the clinic during the raid. At first he thought it was a robbery because the intruders were rifling drawers. But it soon became obvious they were government agents of some kind. Michael demanded to see their identification.

The agents claimed that they didn't have to show anything to anybody. One agent told him, "You'll see our names on the paperwork when we're finished." Michael replied, "No. You demanded IDs from us. I demand to see yours." The agents ignored his demand, even though it's standard procedure for law enforcement officers to display, not conceal, both badges *and* identification.

Michael notified Maureen about the raid, and she immediately alerted Camelot's attorneys. They instructed her to stay home. (She was in fragile health and was no doubt being lured into a trap.) Meanwhile, at the clinic, Michael told the patients that Camelot's legal team was on the way. He informed them, "You don't have to answer any questions."

That infuriated the federal agents.

The agents then tried to command everyone to gather in the lobby while they conducted their search. Michael objected to this and said, "I haven't seen your identification, and I don't consent to being detained. Am I being detained?"

The FBI agent (who had no identification, only a jacket with the letters FBI on it) told Michael, "No." Michael then asked "Then am I free to go?" to which the agent replied, "Yes."

A female agent moved out of his way as he headed for the outside door to leave. Then she suddenly stepped back in his path, causing a collision. The female agent started smiling with glee and pointing at him as he exited the building, yelling to a beefy agent: "Get him! He assaulted me!"

The beefy bully shoved Michael into a concrete wall, bouncing his head on it, then spun him around and slammed him to the ground. Then he drove his knee into Michael's back, nearly crushing him with his tremendous weight. This stunned Michael and drove the breath out of him. He couldn't breathe! The bully resumed his attack and pulled Michael's arm out of the socket, dislocating his left shoulder. Then he cuffed Michael and handed him over to local police.

Michael was such a bloody mess the jail turned him away!

When the Tulsa police took Michael to jail, he was such a bloody mess, the jail refused to accept him until he'd been checked by a hospital emergency room doctor. The ER doctor suspected broken ribs and a possible concussion and other injuries. Michael could barely walk or stand without severe pain. The Tulsa police threw Michael into solitary confinement without access to the medical care he urgently needed.

Incredible as it sounds, Michael spent three days in solitary confinement with *blood in his urine* and without access to medical care. Finally he got a bond hearing and was released.

Fortunately, a patient's husband and another witness swore affidavits describing the facts about the government's attempt to set up Michael. Their affidavits disprove the government's preposterous claim that Michael assaulted the female agent, who in fact beamed with glee after the alleged "assault."

The Feds turn up the heat on Michael

At first, the Feds charged Michael with felony "assault." Later they downgraded the charge to misdemeanor "obstruction." And then the Feds offered Michael a deal. If he would agree to testify against Maureen and Camelot, he would receive partial immunity from prosecution. He would "only" have to plead guilty to a misdemeanor, and he would "only" have to serve one year in federal prison. If he refused, the government threatened to revoke his bond and upgrade his charge back up to a felony, which could mean two years in Club Fed and a $200,000 fine.

Michael stood firm. He refused to knuckle under. He replied, "I don't like your deal. Take me to trial!" That took guts!

Michael knew he hadn't done anything wrong – neither had Maureen nor the Camelot clinic. They're innocent.

But that didn't stop government agents from going on a fishing expedition for more evidence at the office of Maureen's tax attorney. The government demanded e-mails and other documents that are protected by attorney-client privilege. Maureen's attorney told the government agents to take their fishing expedition elsewhere. She wasn't going to violate her ethical obligation to keep attorney-client communications confidential.

The FDA didn't find the "smoking gun" it was looking for

Apparently, the main thing the FBI agents were looking for during their raid was vitamin B17, also known as laetrile. They were acting at the instigation of the FDA, which has declared laetrile an illegal substance and was hoping to seize Camelot's supply of it. The agents found no B17 at Camelot, which poses a problem for the government's case. The agents did, however, find invoices for B17, indicating it had been ordered in the past. At the time of the raid it was on back order.

According to Maureen, she had made no effort to hide the clinic's use of B17, which was a small part of the cancer treatment program at Camelot. The clinic's website and brochures mentioned B17 because she believed this treatment had finally gained acceptance. Maureen told us some mainstream cancer centers, including a well-known national chain of integrative cancer treatment centers, were using B17, one of the ingredients included in "Intravenous Micronutrient Vitamin Pac Infusion." It even has its own ICD-9 code assigned to it, for billing patients' insurance providers: 96365.

If the FDA believes B17 is illegal, it could have just sent Camelot a "cease and desist" letter, demanding that the clinic stop using the remedy. Instead, the agency chose to launch a violent attack.

Of what value is conventional medicine's "free" poison?

The FDA also accuses Camelot of preying on and exploiting desperate cancer patients. This accusation is ironic, considering the FDA protects the conventional cancer treatment industry and authorizes medical experiments in which desperate cancer patients are conned into becoming guinea pigs in human trials of new, unproven cancer drugs.

It's rare for any of these human guinea pigs to survive treatment with these experimental chemotherapy drugs. The unproven drugs are pushed on late-stage cancer patients considered "hopeless" by mainstream medicine, even though alternative medicine frequently reverses such cases and saves the lives of the patients. In contrast, conventional doctors try to enroll such "terminal" patients in drug trials by telling them they can be first in line for a "promising" new treatment.

Consider this: When its doors were still open, Camelot charged only $12,000 for a gentle and effective 20-day round of DMSO-based intravenous treatment. That's a bargain compared to conventional medical treatment. In sharp contrast, conventional doctors and hospitals charge patients as much as $850,000 – and the treatments nearly always fail. Tragically, late-stage patients are charged hundreds of thousands of dollars, only to die of cancer. Who, then, is guilty of preying on and exploiting desperate patients?

Patients may think conventional cancer treatment is "free" because insurance pays for it. But how much is free poison worth? What's more, the conventional treatment racket's failure rate for stage four cancer is nearly 100 percent. To be more exact, its success rate with late-stage cancer is only two out of 100. The other 98 patients are dead within five years. Camelot was beating those odds by a country mile.

Camelot has even cured brain cancer with natural treatments!

Camelot has successfully reversed glioblastoma–brain cancer–one of the deadliest cancers known to man. This is the kind of cancer that killed Senator Ted Kennedy. If Kennedy had come to Camelot for his brain cancer, he might still be alive today. But even with all of his money, he never stood a chance because he chose conventional treatment.

The FDA's Gestapo-like raid dealt Camelot a crippling blow. Without due process of law, the government confiscated all $76,000 of Camelot's operating funds from its bank account, all $51,000 from Maureen's *personal* bank account, and Camelot's office computers, files, and other items. This leaves Camelot unable to continue. The clinic has *no access* to its operating funds. With bank accounts frozen and confiscated, Maureen had no funds to pay the clinic's rent or to pay staff salaries.

It's ironic, but neither the federal government nor the Oklahoma State Medical Board ordered Camelot to be shut down. In theory, Camelot could still be open today. But the sudden seizure of funds, patient records, and office equipment makes it impossible for the clinic to operate. As this report goes to press, the clinic remains closed, and we don't know when, where, or if it will ever reopen. By the time you read this, we hope Camelot will be back in business.

You may find out the status of the clinic by visiting Camelot's website: www.CamelotCancerCare.com.

Chapter Twenty

Other outstanding clinics that offer alternative, holistic, or complementary treatment

Jeanne Drisko, M.D.
Program in Integrative Medicine
University of Kansas Medical Center
3901 Rainbow Boulevard,
Mail Stop 2028
Kansas City, KS 66160
Phone: 913-588-5000
Email: jdrisko@kumc.edu
Website: http://integrativemed.kumc.edu/

Michael Galitzer, M.D.
American Health Institute
12381 Wilshire Boulevard, Suite 102
Los Angeles, CA 90025
Phone: 800-392-2623
Website: www.ahealth.com

Nicholas Gonzalez, M.D.
36A East 36th Street, Suite 204
New York, N.Y. 10016
Phone: 212-213-3337
Website: www.dr-gonzalez.com

Garry Gordon, M.D.
Gordon Research Institute
600 North Beeline Highway, Suite B
Payson, AZ 85541
Phone: 928-472-4263
Website: www.gordonresearch.com

Elson Haas, M.D.
The Preventive Medical Center of Marin
25 Mitchell Boulevard, Suite 8
San Rafael, CA 94903
Phone: 415-472-2343
Email: info@haashealthonline.com
Website: www.elsonhaas.com

Robert Jay Rowen, MD
PO Box 817
Santa Rosa, CA 95402
Phone: 707-578-7787
Email: terrisu@sonic.net
Websites: www.secondopinionnewsletter.com www.doctorrowen.com

Michael Schachter, M.D.
Schachter Center for Complementary Medicine
Two Executive Boulevard, Suite 202
Suffern, New York 10901
Phone: 845-368-4700
Website: www.mbschachter.com

END NOTE

How to choose the right clinic for you or your loved one

Each case of cancer is different. Each doctor is different. And each clinic is different. One size doesn't fit all.

You could check out websites and send emails to the various hospitals, clinics, and doctors we've listed in this Special Report. You could phone the clinics to gather more information. But many people don't have the time or the patience to call several clinics or to wait for email responses.

Because I know the doctors, the clinics, the hospitals, and the various treatment options, some people have sought my advice as a "cancer coach." I'm now helping many people this way on a professional basis. I'd be glad to help you, too, find the right clinic.

Any treatment decisions you make, of course, are entirely your responsibility. I'm not a doctor. But I do have a great deal of information and I'd be happy to share it with you.

I'd be glad to help you learn about the clinics in more depth. If you'd like my help, please contact me at the phone number or email address below. And since you purchased this Special Report, we'll give you a $25.00 discount off my services (regularly $150.00 per hour). To get the discount, just mention that you bought the Special Report.

You can reach me through my wife, Chayo, who schedules my consultations. Chayo is super friendly. She really likes people, and I know you'll enjoy talking with her. Here is our contact information:

Phone: 209-529-4697

Email: frankcousineau@sbcglobal.net

Please don't hesitate to leave a voicemail message if Chayo is away from her desk or on the phone. If you prefer you can contact me directly by email: frankcousineau@sbcglobal.net.